The Girls

of

Everly Hall

Cindy S. Hill

by Cindy S. Hill

For the Girls

Prologue

My name is Laramie Johnson. When I was 15 years old, I made a mistake. It could have destroyed me, but instead it turned my life around for the better. I owe it all to two special people who started something great and passed on the legacy to the next generation.

This is my story.

Georgia and Francis Everly dreamt of having a family of their own someday. But Georgia's health issues shattered those dreams.

When Francis was approached by a wealthy investor about buying his sawmill, new opportunities opened for the Everlys.

With a desire to help unwed teenage mothers, they immediately started the Everly Foundation. Using the income from the sale of the business to purchase property and remodel an existing building, they opened the Everly Hall School for Girls. The home provided safety and security for girls in unfortunate circumstances.

When businessmen and charity groups learned of the good the Everlys were doing, they were willing to invest in the foundation.

Thanks to constant income from outside sources, no girl was ever required to pay for assistance from Everly Hall.

The first resident at Everly Hall would change the lives of the Everlys forever.

How did her gift enrich their lives and mine?

Chapter 1: Meet the Everlys

Francis and Georgia Everly met when they were juniors in high school.

Theirs was the typical high school romance - Francis the handsome jock and Georgia, the beautiful head cheerleader.

They personified the perfect high school couple and were voted Jr. Prom King and Queen.

Francis' parents were the wealthy owners of the town sawmill in Boston. Tragically, during his senior year, Francis' father died in a fire that started when a pile of lumber dust resting next to steam pipes erupted into flames.

Everyone had gone home for the night.

The alarm hadn't been activated, and the firefighters didn't arrive until the fire extensively damaged the facility.

When Mr. Everly saw the black smoke pouring out of the sawmill, he and his wife rushed to see what was going on.

Mr. Everly tried putting the fire out by himself but was consumed by the flames. While trying to rescue her husband, Mrs. Everly suffered smoke inhalation that damaged her lungs.

When the firefighters finally arrived at the scene, they found Mr. Everly dead and his wife barely alive. Francis was devastated by his father's loss and quit high school to help his mother.

As the only child, Francis grew up fast by learning to run the family business. The fire not only killed his father but also destroyed Francis' high school football days and dreams of a college scholarship. Georgia stayed by his side and supported whatever decisions he made.

She finished her senior year of high school and went on to college in nearby Hanover. They remained sweethearts throughout a long-distance relationship and often traveled the three hours to visit on the weekends.

After Georgia graduated with her bachelor's degree in business, she returned home to Francis in Boston.

Francis stayed busy running the mill, but realized his real love was Georgia. He wanted to spend the rest of his life with her by his side. He decided they should get married.

Georgia agreed it was time.

Georgia's parents were excited that their only child was finally getting married. They were happy to see their daughter settle down and start a family.

It was rare in 1925 for a girl her age to still be single. It was almost as unusual and quite shocking for a woman to graduate from college in those days.

Francis and Georgia got married on October 14, 1926, in Stoneham, Maine.

They found the perfect spot while driving to see the autumn leaves one Sunday afternoon. It was a beautiful array of red, orange and yellow trees set along the edge of the lake. As their loved ones looked on, the newlyweds imagined themselves living somewhere just like it one day.

The day was perfect.

Georgia wanted to have children right away. Francis was reluctant about providing for a family but was willing to do his part in the effort.

Month after month went by with the same sad news – no baby was on the way.

Each time Georgia got herself worked up about being pregnant only to be met with massive disappointment. Francis didn't know how to comfort her.

He was busy with work and thought about other things, while Georgia's mind constantly wrestled with the sad realization that a family might not be in their future.

After nearly a year with no success, Francis' mother suggested Georgia see an infertility doctor.

The idea was frightening to the Everlys. They had always pictured themselves with a house full of laughing, rambunctious children.

The ability to conceive wasn't openly discussed with family and friends, but the couple was open to suggestions on the subject.

A new obstetrician recently opened a practice in Boston, and he was getting rave reviews from the local women. Georgia scheduled an appointment to see the doctor.

He was a kind man who seemed to genuinely care about Georgia's concerns. He suggested Georgia try glandular extracts to improve her chances of ovulating. If that didn't work, he really had no other options at this point other than running multiple tests.

Francis and Georgia weren't quite ready for that step yet, but Georgia agreed to try the hormone stimulants.

Another six months went by without a pregnancy. Tests confirmed that Georgia could not carry a child as a cervix blockage prevented her from conceiving.

The news devastated the couple, but Georgia felt particularly sad about the situation. Their dreams for the future were gone, and it appeared for good.

Georgia had to find something to occupy her time. Since she couldn't have children of her own, she wanted to help others.

During her visits to the doctor, Georgia noticed many unwed teenage mothers. She wondered if there was something she could do for them.

Georgia prepared to present her idea to Francis.

That same day, Francis was offered a generous amount of money for the sawmill. He wasn't sure he should accept the offer and planned to discuss it with Georgia over dinner. When he arrived home to a candlelight table for two, he wasn't quite sure what to think.

"What's this all about?" he inquired.

Georgia approached him with open arms.

"Can't a wife make a special dinner for her sweetheart without being suspected of something?" she asked.

"Well, I'll take it under any circumstances, but I must admit it's got me curious," Francis said.

"Sit down and enjoy your meal, Mr. Everly. I do have something I want to discuss with you," Georgia said as she winked at her husband.

"I knew you were up to something, Mrs. Everly," he mused, as he sat down at the elaborately decorated table. "As a matter of fact, there is an item of business I'd like to discuss with you too."

"Oh, you've piqued my attention now. You go first." Georgia said eagerly as she placed some food on his plate.

"I was approached by an investor today, who is interested in purchasing the sawmill. He made a very tempting offer. I'm curious how you would feel about selling it?" Francis asked.

Georgia gasped.

"I'm surprised to hear that," she said. "I wasn't aware you were thinking about selling. Thank you for including me in such a decision."

"Of course, I would consider your feelings," he replied. "Well, what are your thoughts?"

Georgia took a deep breath.

"Strange that you should ask…I've been having thoughts of my own. Since we aren't going to be able to have children," she paused while collecting her emotions. "I have come up with an idea to help occupy my time."

"Go on. I'm listening," he said.

"I would like to help unwed, pregnant teens," she continued. "Selling the business would certainly help out my cause."

"What did you have in mind?" Francis asked inquisitively.

The two of them went on to discuss both propositions and what it all would entail. They decided to accept the offer and proceed with forming a foundation for unwed mothers. After paying off their existing bills, they could use the leftover funds.

The first step would be finding land to purchase for an unwed mother's home.

For inspiration, the Everlys took a day and drove to the mountains where they got married. To their surprise there was a "For Sale" sign posted in the field.

They couldn't believe it! They wrote down the contact information of the realtor and drove to the nearest phone booth.

The agent was available to see them that afternoon. To their delight, the amount wanted for the property was nearly equal to what they had saved.

Georgia's parents were more than happy to cover the remaining balance. There was an older building on the property that could easily be renovated that the owner agreed to throw in at no additional cost to the Everlys.

Francis and Georgia immediately went to work on the house. They salvaged most of the materials and remodeled the rooms and dining room.

They could make additional changes as needed later.

Now to find tenants for the Everly Hall School for Girls.

The seasons changed and snow began to fall.

The construction crew temporarily ceased operations while waiting for the snow to melt.

One day, Mr. Everly went into town to finalize some of the paperwork for the Everly Foundation when he noticed a commotion across the street.

He approached a small group of men huddled around another man holding something.

"Let me through," announced a gentleman carrying a black medical bag.

"What have we here?" he calmly said.

He gently unwrapped the overcoat to expose a young boy's frozen face. He felt for a pulse. He shook his head, and the man holding the child wept uncontrollably.

Francis moved forward to help support the man's shaking body. Francis helped the sobbing man inside the nearby grocery store and sat him on the bench near the wood stove to warm up.

"Is there someone we can contact for you?" he gently asked.

"Yes, my wife, Dorothy King," the man mumbled through his tears. "We live just down the road on Myrtle Street."

Francis ran down the snow-covered street and turned at the intersection marked "Myrtle Street."

"Dorothy, Dorothy King!" Francis frantically yelled.

A young girl peered out her front door and asked what he wanted with her mother. Francis cautiously approached her and explained the situation.

Shocked, she and Dorothy listened as he described the scene he walked into.

Francis said he would take them to their husband, father and brother, but Dorothy refused to move. The young girl put her boots and coat on and followed as Francis carried Dorothy to the grocery store.

Once he delivered them safely to Mr. King, Francis left the family alone to mourn.

The boy's obituary appeared in the town newspaper, and Francis wanted to pay his respects.

He traveled to the cemetery and observed from afar. He didn't want to disturb the family during this time of grief.

As the service ended, Francis noticed the girl sobbing uncontrollably. Her father was consoling her mother and was oblivious to his daughter's sorrow.

Francis walked up behind the young girl and tapped her on the shoulder offering his arms in comfort. She recognized his face and gave in to her sadness.

Progress on the Everlys' property and lodge continued in the spring and neared completion.

Hoping to attract unwed mothers to the Everlys' home, Georgia had reached out to unwed mothers at doctor's offices. Despite her efforts, the girls hesitated to move into a home with strangers.

Over a year had passed since the death of the young boy. The Great Depression had hit hard, and Francis knew everyone had not been as fortunate as he and his wife. He decided to make a visit and check on the King family.

Francis knocked on the King's front door and nervously waited. He wasn't really sure what he was going to say.

Slowly, Dorothy King opened the door. She had no recollection of who Francis was.

"Can I help you?" she asked.

The young girl appeared around the corner, wearing a loose housecoat. She immediately recognized him and introduced him to her mother as a friend of her father's.

Francis explained the reason for his visit. Conrad King came from the kitchen, visibly upset about having to wait for his dinner thanks to the unexpected guest. Francis asked how they were doing.

Very agitated, Conrad announced that his daughter was pregnant and stormed out of the room. The girl apologized for her father's behavior and suggested it was time for Francis to go. He handed her his business card and said to call if they ever needed anything.

The next morning, Francis got a phone call from Edna.

"Were you serious about helping out if there ever was a need?" she asked cautiously.

"Of course," he replied. "How can I be of service?"

"I could use a place to live," she answered.

She explained that she was pregnant, and her mother wasn't well. They discussed what the Everlys had to offer.

Francis was anxious to tell Georgia what had transpired. After hanging up with Edna, he quickly had his secretary get his wife on the line.

Georgia answered the telephone, and before she could even say "hello," Francis exploded with enthusiasm.

"We have our first client!" he blurted.

"What are you talking about?" she asked, confused.

Francis told her about his recent conversation with Edna King.

"Well, we have a lot to do then," she responded.

"Yes, we do," Francis said. "She arrives in the morning."

The next day, a driver arrived at Dorothy and Conrad King's home to pick up Edna.

She hugged her parents one last time and rode away to the Everly Hall School for Girls.

Edna King

Chapter 2: Meet Edna King

In the midst of the Great Depression, on a cold, wintry November night in 1934, a baby girl was born.

The baby's father, Conrad, had recently lost his bank job and could not afford to take the baby's mother, Dorothy, to the hospital.

It had been a difficult pregnancy with constant morning sickness coupled with a lot of cramping and bleeding.

When Dorothy went into labor, she and Conrad were both beyond scared.

Dorothy had suffered a miscarriage a year before, and they had been especially careful during this second pregnancy.

Conrad really wanted Dorothy to be under a doctor's care, but there was barely enough money to buy groceries. Yet, they felt fortunate to have found a midwife living close by. She had been by the house a couple of times to check on Dorothy.

After hours of contractions, Dorothy's water broke. Conrad put on his ragged, worn-out coat and raced through the heavy snowstorm to the midwife's home.

As he stood shivering in the cold, he banged loudly on the front door.

"Please, help me!" he yelled. "My wife is in labor!"

Conrad knocked on the door again. Finally, the midwife came to the door and let Conrad in.

"We've got to hurry! The baby is coming!" Conrad said through chattering teeth.

"You must calm down, Mr. King," the midwife said. "A frantic husband cannot help his wife. Sit down while I gather my things. We can take my car back to your house."

The midwife slowly walked through her small apartment and returned with a black bag.

"We can go now," she calmly said.

The midwife led Conrad to her car that was parked on the street. They climbed in, and, as the midwife started the cold car, it sputtered and sputtered then sputtered again.

Conrad nervously leaned back and forth in the car's front seat.

I'm going to run back home. It would be faster, he thought.

Much to Conrad's relief, the car finally started.

Soon the car was humming along as they drove to Conrad's house.

Conrad burst into his home followed by the ever-serene midwife. There they found Dorothy in active labor holding on to the side of the kitchen table rocking back and forth.

Despite how cold it was in the apartment, sweat rolled down Dorothy's forehead.

"There, there," said the midwife as she approached Dorothy. "You're going to be just fine."

Conrad put his arm around his wife's shoulder as he and the midwife helped Dorothy to the bedroom.

Earlier that day, Conrad had put clean sheets on the bed.

If I can't provide a hospital bed for her, I can make the most of what we've got, he thought as he made up the bed.

Dorothy screamed as she collapsed onto the bed.

"We must be getting close," the midwife said.

The midwife was finally showing some real concern.

"Mr. King, get some hot water and clean towels," she ordered as she pointed Conrad toward the kitchen.

Conrad hesitated but did as he was told. He went into the kitchen and boiled some water. He found clean, white towels and took them to the bedroom.

Conrad felt so helpless as he stood nearby watching his wife in such distress.

The teapot's whistle interrupted Conrad's thoughts. He quickly went into the kitchen, grabbed the teapot's handle and shrieked. He shook his hand as the midwife ran to his side. He shooed her away to go tend to his wife.

Conrad quickly walked over to the kitchen sink and let the cold water pour over his aching burned hand. When the pain subsided, Conrad reached for a hot pad and carried the teapot to the bedroom.

Dorothy panted heavily as she focused on each impending contraction. The midwife placed her hands under the sheets and felt the baby's head coming.

"One more big push, Mrs. King. Your baby is almost here," the midwife said slowly and in soft soothing tones.

Dorothy wailed as she pushed the baby into the world.

Soon the unrelenting sound of the baby's first cry filled the small apartment.

Conrad ran to Dorothy's side, and they embraced as new parents for the first time.

They chose the name, Edna, because she brought them pleasure and delight. The midwife gave the baby girl a thorough check.

"She's perfect, Dorothy," the midwife said as she placed the new baby girl on Dorothy's breast. The midwife quietly left the new family alone.

******

The Great Depression proved a struggle for most families, but Conrad was fortunate to get his banking job back. His hours were cut, and his wages were as low as 50 cents an hour, but at least he had a job, the couple agreed.

Dorothy took in sewing and mending to help with expenses.

When Edna was four years old, Dorothy gave birth to a baby boy the Kings named Frankie.

Despite Edna's very young age, the responsibility of taking care of Frankie fell to her.

It had been a difficult delivery, and Dorothy had lost a significant amount of blood. Sadly, Dorothy couldn't have any more children after Frankie was born.

Dorothy was warned that future pregnancies could kill her. The news broke her heart and caused Dorothy to plunge into a constant state of sadness the doctors described as "depressive disorder."

Dorothy couldn't function for days on end.

Occasionally, she had a good day, and on those days, she took Edna and Frankie for a walk or to the park. During those rare moments, Edna got to be a little girl for a few short hours and enjoyed playing with her mother and younger brother.

Depressive disorder was still new in the 1930s, and most doctors were not familiar with the diagnosis let alone how to treat it.

Trying to avoid shock treatments and long-term stays in a mental hospital, Conrad searched for a doctor who might offer hope in another way.

Conrad learned of a new drug meant to alter the chemicals in Dorothy's brain.

He located a doctor willing to prescribe the medication just as long as he could follow up with Dorothy on a monthly basis.

At first the results were subtle, where Dorothy played on the floor with Frankie for a few minutes each day. Sometimes she hummed a favorite melody.

Edna relished the happy moments and took advantage of the time by herself. Instead of grownup duties like changing Frankie's diapers, Edna played with her dolls and sang them lullabies. Rather than doing the dishes, she had tea parties with her imaginary friends.

Only thin curtains separated the rooms in the tiny apartment, not leaving much room for privacy. Edna always played in a corner of her bedroom, so she could be as far away as possible.

She wasn't allowed to go outside by herself as her momma wanted to see where Edna was all the time.

When Dorothy fell into another depressive state, Edna stayed close by to keep Frankie safe.

Once Dorothy left Frankie alone near the wood stove. He had just learned to crawl and was intrigued by the red flames glowing between the cracks.

His chubby little hand stretched forward just as Edna came into the room and rescued him. Dorothy was in the other room oblivious to what had happened. It was never mentioned to her or to Conrad.

Everyone agreed, it was important to keep the family together, but child protection services watched the Kings closely. Anytime a psychotic patient was kept in the home, child protection considered it dangerous. Conrad repeatedly assured them that the children were safe and cared for - even if that meant a six-year-old child was the baby's caregiver.

After years of treatment, Dorothy started taking care of her children.

Conrad's hours at the bank were increased, but the family still lived frugally.

When Edna started attending school, she never invited friends over because she was too embarrassed by their living conditions. She and Frankie were very close and spent a lot of time together playing make-believe. They pretended to go to the moon, or to be rich and to travel the world.

Edna checked out books from the school library and brought them home to read to Frankie. The stories would take them to far-away places where they escaped the reality of their own lives.

At night, with only the light from their oil lamps, Edna made tents out of sheets and acted as if they were going on a wild adventure. They went to Africa on a wildlife safari or to New York City to see a Broadway show.

Edna made shadow figures on the tent walls to make it more lifelike. Yet, when the sun came through the windows, the adventures sadly ended.

When Frankie was about 11 years old, he decided to take a real-life journey without telling anyone he was going. Tired of pretending, Frankie wanted to see what the world was really like beyond his apartment and schoolhouse.

After school, Edna wanted to go to a friend's house and told Frankie to walk home alone. Now that she was 15, she would often leave him and find more grown-up things to occupy her time. She still loved Frankie but wanted some time for herself and her friends.

Frankie took this as an opportunity to go exploring. So, instead of turning right to head in the direction of home, he went left. He decided to alternate by turning left then right. He didn't really know where he was going. He just wanted to go somewhere.

As the night drew darker, Frankie realized he had no idea where he was, or which direction home was.

He was cold.

He was hungry.

He had eaten an apple for lunch hours earlier, but now his stomach growled with hunger.

Not knowing what else to do, Frankie hunkered down in a corner next to a grocery store and wrapped himself in his thin overcoat. He found some brown paper bags nearby and placed them between himself and the sidewalk.

Snow poured down upon him like powdered sugar on a donut.

"I would love a donut right now," Frankie thought.

Frankie closed his eyes and dreamt of danishes and pastries lining the streets of Europe just like in the stories Edna read to him. Soon he was sound asleep. The snow continued falling all night, but Frankie was too cold to move.

Morning never came for Frankie.

The grocery store owner arrived by eight that day to greet the morning shoppers.

As he approached the front door, the grocer noticed something in the corner.

"Oh, my goodness!" he gasped, as he revealed the frozen body underneath the snow-covered jacket. He carefully picked him up and screamed for help.

The men who had gathered for morning coffee, raced to the store to see what all the yelling was about.

Conrad's bank was across the street from the grocery store, and he was just arriving for work. Seeing the commotion, Conrad looked both ways, then ran across the street.

"What is going on here?" he asked.

The grocery store owner told someone to get a doctor. Conrad got closer to see what the store owner was holding. Another man helped steady Conrad when he realized the snow-covered body was his Frankie! Without thinking, Conrad yanked the frozen body from the man's arms and sobbed violently.

"No, this can't be," he kept repeating while rocking Frankie's body in his arms, back and forth, back and forth.

Finally, the doctor arrived.

"Let me have a look," the doctor calmly said.

Pulling the coat away from Frankie's face, the doctor immediately knew that Frankie was gone.

The doctor gently covered Frankie up again and shook his head at the others.

Conrad fell to the ground moaning in grief. An unknown man wrapped father and son in his arms and tightly held them until Conrad could cry no more.

Then the man carefully helped Conrad up and walked him inside the grocery store to warm himself on a bench near a wood stove.

"Is there someone we can get for you, sir?" the gentleman asked.

"My wife, Dorothy King. We live just a few blocks from here on Myrtle Street," Conrad mumbled.

The stranger quickly got up and ran toward Myrtle Street. When he got to the intersection, he began yelling, "Dorothy, Dorothy King!"

Edna and her mother huddled inside their home near their fireplace.

With Frankie not coming home from school, they stayed awake all night worrying and waiting for his return.

Edna heard the man calling for Dorothy in the distance. She glanced out the window to see him running up and down the street shouting her mother's name.

Edna flung open the front door.

"We're here, inside. What's going on?" Edna asked.

"Are you Dorothy King?" the man asked reluctantly. "No, but she is my mother. I repeat, what is going on?"

"I'm afraid I have some bad news," he said. "A young boy was found outside the grocery store this morning and...and he is dead."

"What has that got to do with us?" a shocked Edna asked.

The kind man reached for her hand.

"We believe it is your brother, Frankie. Your father is with him and asked me to get your mother. I can take you to them," the man said.

Dorothy listened from inside, refusing to believe that her Frankie was dead.

"Frankie is on his way home now," Dorothy insisted. "He should be home any minute."

She refused to move off the couch.

Finally, the man lifted Dorothy and wrapped her in a blanket he grabbed off the back of a nearby chair. Edna put on her coat and boots and walked through the snow with her mother and the man toward the grocery store.

The days leading up to the funeral were a struggle just to get through.

Dorothy's mental health deteriorated drastically following Frankie's death. Her doctor prescribed anti-anxiety medication to help calm Dorothy's nerves. It failed to help, and the doctors finally gave her Valium so she could get some much-needed rest.

With Conrad not wanting to leave her alone, the funeral arrangements were left up to Edna. She organized a small family gathering at the cemetery with the town pastor saying some final words.

Dorothy was in attendance, but only physically. She stared blankly at her son's casket.

Conrad and Edna stood on both sides of Dorothy and helped her to the casket to say "goodbye" to Frankie.

Dorothy slowly went through the motions as tears cascaded down her cheeks.

Edna took the blame for Frankie's death.

"I should have been there to walk him home," she repeatedly berated herself.

The sorrow became unbearable for Edna. There was no one to help her.

Her father could only comfort his wife.

From behind her, Edna felt an arm around her shoulders.

She turned to see the face of the kind gentleman who had been with them the day they found Frankie's body. Edna succumbed to his embrace and let the tears fall freely.

Sometime later, the family returned to their car and went home. That day was never spoken of again.

Dorothy was never the same after Frankie's death. Edna became the caregiver, only now she was in high school and had other interests.

After school each day, Edna came home to give Dorothy her meds before preparing dinner.

When her father got home, they sat and ate dinner while listening to "Fibber McGee and Molly" on the radio.

Occasionally, one of them would chuckle and break the awkward silence.

But no words were ever exchanged. Edna would clean up the dishes and then go to a friend's house to do homework.

On the weekends, Edna attended parties and went to dances at the town hall. The dances were for ages 18 and up, and she was only 16.

She had friends who knew the bouncer, and he let her in.

Edna loved putting on her momma's make-up and pretending to be someone else for the night. Her momma hadn't been out in a while and had a closet full of party dresses she never wore.

Conrad bought them for her in an attempt to cheer her up, but it didn't work.

Edna had grown into a pretty, young woman, and her mother's dresses looked dashing on her. Her friends were jealous of her for the first time in her life, and Edna gloated at the irony of it all.

On the one-year anniversary of Frankie's death, Edna decided to go out instead of staying in with her parents. There was a dance she wanted to attend.

Boys were coming in from the nearby college, and she was anxious to meet them. She walked to town alone, but assured her parents that a friend could bring her home.

The dance hall was filled with heavy cigarette smoke and the stench of alcohol - even more so tonight.

More than one rule was being broken.

Young men roamed like hungry lions looking for their prey. There was one especially good-looking guy who kept walking by Edna and her friends.

"Why don't you just ask her to dance already?" one of Edna's friends finally asked.

He acted surprised and turned around.

"Who, me?" he replied.

"Yes, you. You know you want to," the friend said.

The young man grabbed Edna by the arm and twirled her onto the dance floor. Soon Edna realized she was having a really good time. Before she knew it, they had been on the dance floor for nearly an hour.

The liquor on his breath was almost too much for her, but his chiseled jawbone and well-sculpted chest somehow made it easier to bear.

She found herself swept up in the moment. He put his hand on her back and led her out to the parking lot and into his truck. She sunk into his arms, overcome with emotion.

"What's the matter?" he asked as he pretended to care.

"Today marks one year since my brother's passing," Edna replied, fighting back the tears.

"I'll make all the sadness go away," he smirked.

Edna fell under his spell and let herself travel to a far-off place just like she and Frankie used to do. When she came out of her trance, she was alone in the truck.

Scared of what just happened, she climbed out of the truck and staggered back into the dance hall. Her friends were at a table staring at her.

"Did you have a good time?" they teased.

Just then she saw the boy walk out with a different girl on his arm.

"Get me out of here, now!" Edna cried.

Her so-called friends just laughed and told her to find her own way home.

Edna turned and slowly walked out of the dance hall into the dark and lonely night.

Months went by with no word of that night ever happening. Edna stayed home from the dances and parties to take care of her mother.

Her friends would come by to get her, but eventually they stopped.

One evening, she felt particularly lonely and very nauseous. She barely made it to the bathroom before losing her dinner in the toilet.

"What is wrong with me?" she asked herself.

Noticing the unopened package of sanitary pads under the sink, Edna realized she hadn't had a period in two months. Being so consumed with her mother, Edna had lost track of time. Her mind went back to that dreadful night at the dance hall.

"It can't be," she uttered.

A visit to the free women's clinic confirmed her suspicions. Edna knew her parents would be so disappointed, and it would worsen her mother's mental health. But she also knew she had to tell them. She wasn't sure how, or when, but she had to let them know.

Edna waited as long as she could before telling her parents. At least it was summer break, and she didn't have to go to school.

When she could no longer hide her growing stomach, Edna approached her parents after dinner and right before they turned on the radio.

"Momma, Daddy, I need to tell you both something," she whimpered. "I know you will be angry and disappointed in me. Do you remember the night I walked home from the dance alone? Well, something awful happened to me that night. I was sad and lonely…and I fell for what I thought was someone who cared about me. But, instead, he just used me for his own selfish desires."

She started to sob and could barely speak. She looked into her parents' concerned eyes.

"I'm pregnant," Edna cried.

No other words were spoken, and Edna left the room.

Several days later there was a knock at the door. When Dorothy opened it, there stood the man who always seemed to show up when he was needed.

"How may I help you?" she asked.

Dorothy had no recollection of him. Her manic episodes combined with her medication, made her very forgetful.

Edna walked into the living room wearing an oversized house dress.

"I am Mr. Francis Everly," he answered. "I helped you the day your son was found."

Dorothy had no idea what he was referring to and stared at him with little expression on her face.

"I thought I recognized you," Edna said as she quickly cut in and spoke softly to her mother. "Momma, this is a friend of daddy's."

"It's been a while, and I thought I would check in and see how your family is doing. Times have been hard on folks," Francis said.

Conrad came to see what was holding up his dinner and saw Francis standing there in his fancy suit.

"Well, I can tell you how we are!" Conrad said. "Our son is dead, my wife isn't well, and now our only daughter has gone off and gotten herself pregnant!"

Edna gasped and put a hand over her mouth.

Mr. Everly stood silently staring at Conrad.

"Mr. Everly, I am sorry for my father's rudeness," Edna said. "You have always been so kind to us. This has nothing to do with you. Thank you for stopping by."

"If you ever need anything, please don't hesitate to call me," Mr. Everly said as he handed his business card to Edna and let himself out.

The next day, Edna walked to the nearest phone booth and asked the operator to reach Mr. Everly for her. She gave the operator the number and waited for someone to pick up.

"Everly Hall Foundation, how may I direct your call," a woman asked.

Edna was not expecting that.

"May I speak to Mr. Everly?" Edna asked.

After a brief hold, Francis answered the other end of the line.

"This is Mr. Francis Everly," he said.

Edna froze for a moment, forgetting why she called.

"Hello?" he said.

Edna cleared her throat.

"I am sorry to bother you," she said. "This is Edna King. You left your card with me yesterday."

"Oh, yes. Miss King, what can I do for you?" he asked.

"Did you mean it when you said to let you know if I ever needed anything?" Edna asked.

"Of course, I did. Do you need something?" he answered.

Edna hesitated for a moment but suddenly blurted out, "Yes, I could use a place to live."

The conversation continued with a lot of questions, and finally they both said goodbye. Edna returned home to pack her bags.

The next morning, a driver came to pick her up.

Dorothy and Conrad gave their daughter one final hug.

Edna disappeared from their sight.

Chapter 3: A Fresh Start

Edna sat in the back seat of the car staring blankly out the window of the black limousine.

She had no idea where she was going.

A total stranger was driving her to an unknown destination.

"What part of this makes any sense?" she questioned under her breath.

Searching for the right button to press, she waited for an answer.

"May I help you?" a man with a deep voice asked.

"Sir, can you tell me how long the drive will be? I'm feeling a bit nauseous back here," Edna said.

"I can pull over and let you out, if you'd like to get some fresh air, miss," he said.

Edna nodded in agreement as the driver came to a halt. He quickly opened her door. Edna jumped out and vomited on the grass, narrowly missing the driver's shiny, black shoes.

"I am so sorry," she said as she wiped her face.

"Not a problem, Miss Edna," he said. "Would you like to ride up front for the rest of the journey? The road will be very windy and may upset your stomach."

Edna had never met, much less spoken to a colored man. It made her a little nervous, but she trusted that Mr. Everly would not endanger her or her unborn baby.

"Yes, I would like that. Thank you," she said.

"My name is Edmond, ma'am. Shall we carry on?" he asked.

The two of them got back into the limousine and continued up the mountain. It was a steep climb with lots of turns. The road signs warned of the curves ahead, and Edna was grateful to be in the front seat.

Feeling extra tired, Edna drifted off to sleep.

When she opened her eyes, Edna saw she was surrounded by forest. She blinked several times to clear her vision.

It was the most beautiful place she had ever seen.

Edmond let her out of the car and removed her luggage from the trunk.

"This way, Miss Edna," he motioned.

Edna followed Edmond up the cobblestone path to the front porch. Hanging from the edge of the house was a freshly painted sign reading, "Everly Hall School for Girls."

Georgia Everly stepped out with open arms to welcome Edna.

"We are so glad you are here, Edna," Georgia said. "Nice to meet you. Mr. Everly has told me all about you."

"Thank you for having me, Mrs. Everly," Edna said as she held back tears. "I didn't know what to do, or where to go."

"Let's get you settled," Georgia said. "You must be tired from the drive."

Edna went to gather her bags but realized Edmond had already taken them for her.
Georgia directed her down the hall to her room. She opened the door to reveal her new home.

"Welcome home," Georgia announced.

Edna entered the room and placed her suitcase on the bed. She looked around at her new surroundings and felt great gratitude for such a safe place to live.

Edna collapsed onto the bed where she quickly fell into a peaceful sleep.

A few hours later, a knock on her door startled Edna awake.

"It's time for dinner," a familiar voice called.

It was Francis Everly.

Edna was excited to see him again. She opened the door and gave him a big hug.

Dinner was served in a large dining room arranged for several people to eat at the same time. Realizing that she was the only girl there, Edna asked, "Where are the other girls?" Georgia Everly looked at her husband.

"You are our first resident, Edna," Georgia said. "We hope you will be happy here as you make this your new home. We look forward to helping lots of girls in the future."

A little stunned, Edna finished her dinner and asked if she could retire for the night. Getting a nod, she went to her room.

After putting her clothes away and brushing her teeth, Edna climbed into the murphy bed and peacefully drifted away into dreamland.

The following days were filled with exploring the Everly Hall's grounds and getting acquainted with Francis and Georgia.

Mr. Everly returned to Boston to do some work with the foundation.

"I may have a surprise for you when I come back," he announced, as he drove away with Edmond.

Three days later, Georgia and Edna heard Francis' limo coming up the gravel driveway. They ran to welcome him home.

They were delighted when Edmond opened the limo's back door to reveal two girls, Lettie and Miriam. They appeared to be about the same age as Edna, and also had protruding tummies.

Happy to have company, Edna ran to greet the new girls with open arms.

They stood back in reluctance, and she held off a little until they were ready. Trust was something that had to be earned - especially in this situation.

Edmond showed the girls to their rooms. For now, they each had their own room. Hopefully, that would change as more girls arrived.

Each day was more exciting than the one before. As the girls shared their stories, friendships were formed, and they learned to confide in each other.

They had all been deceived by someone they thought cared about them.

Learning to trust again was going to take some time. They each had big decisions to make regarding their unborn babies.

Miriam was nearly seven months along and was thinking of keeping her baby. Her parents had agreed to raise him as their own.

She would go through life pretending to be his older sister. That way she could still watch him grow up without suffering the stigma of unwed motherhood.

Lettie was due any day. She decided to place her baby for adoption.

As part of their services, Francis found a couple and arranged the adoption through a local law agency.

It would be a closed adoption, and Lettie would never see her baby again.

That idea terrified Edna, but she still hadn't made a decision.

The girls were kept comfortable but were required to perform tasks each day. With only three of them, they stayed quite busy.

There was a rotating chore chart that kept track of their daily responsibilities. By the end of the day, they were tired and ready for bed.

When Lettie didn't show up for breakfast one morning, Edna checked on her. She found Lettie lying on the floor, moaning.

"We need help!" Edna screamed.

Georgia came running and told Miriam to call the hospital immediately.

Lettie let out a shriek and doubled over in pain.

The ambulance didn't make it in time. Lettie's baby was born minutes later.

Lettie refused to look at her baby, let alone hold her.

The ambulance finally arrived and took her and the baby to the hospital.

Georgia rode along to comfort Lettie.

They never saw Lettie or the baby again.

Edna felt butterflies in her stomach while she lay resting one afternoon.

Suddenly a thump hit her from inside her belly. She jumped in surprise.

"Mrs. Everly," she cried. "Come quick! Something is wrong!"

Georgia quickly arrived at her side and gently placed her hand on Edna's swollen tummy.

"Everything is just fine. Your baby is kicking," Georgia chuckled.

Edna sighed in relief and put her hands over her restless stomach.

Miriam went into labor during the night, and Francis drove her to the hospital. She delivered a healthy, baby boy.

Miriam's parents were by her side, and their names were put on the birth certificate as the baby's mother and father. No one would ever know the truth.

******

With Miriam and Lettie both gone, Edna had a lot of time to think. After watching what went on with the other girls, at least Edna knew what she didn't want.

But what were her other options?

Even with all the work the foundation was doing, Georgia and Francis still felt an emptiness in their lives. The thought crossed their minds that maybe they could adopt Edna's baby.

The couple decided to present the idea to her.

"Edna, we would like to discuss something with you," Georgia said, while they were doing the dinner dishes.

"Have I done anything wrong?" a worried Edna asked.

"Oh no, nothing's wrong," Georgia said. "We have a proposition for you."

Georgia and Francis sat holding hands across the living room from Edna.

She sat nervously, fidgeting in her chair. Finding a comfortable position was getting harder and harder every day.

"Edna, have you made a decision about your baby?" Georgia asked.

Edna shook her head.

"Well, we would like to…adopt your baby," Georgia gingerly said. "That is, if you'll agree to it."

Edna sat stunned. She wasn't sure what to say.

The room suddenly fell silent as a million thoughts swirled through Edna's mind. She thought of the other two pregnant girls, and the decisions they had made.

After a few moments of silence, she replied.

"I would like that very much," Edna said softly.

The legal papers were quickly drawn up and work began on the nursery just as fast. The baby was due in a few weeks, and there was much to do.

It was decided that the room would be painted pale yellow to accommodate either a boy or a girl.

Edna practiced her sewing skills and made the curtains. Georgia's mother pieced together a patchwork quilt while Francis' mother made burp cloths and diapers.

Francis and Georgia took a day trip into Boston and purchased a crib and a small dresser.

Everything was ready for the baby to arrive.

That night Edna awoke suddenly and found herself lying atop soaked sheets.

"Did I wet my pants?" she asked herself.

She felt a slight twinge in her abdomen, followed by a severe cramping sensation.

"Ouch! You don't have to kick so hard," Edna said to the unborn baby.

That was followed by another cramp and more pain this time.

Edna staggered out of bed and crawled to the door. Pushing it open, she yelled as loud as she was able.

"Help me, please!" She cried as another pain seared across her back.

Georgia and Francis raced down the hall.

"Let's get you to the hospital!" Georgia said. "We're having a baby!"

A few hours later, a baby girl was born.

The Everlys went to the hospital nursery to get the first look at their new daughter.

She had a little round face, and black hair covered her tiny head. They couldn't wait to hold her. Edna was exhausted and sleeping in her hospital bed nearby.

Two days later they all returned home as a family.

A large oak tree grew outside the window of the nursery, so they agreed on the name, "Oakley" for the Everlys' new baby girl.

Years went by, and Oakley grew into a beautiful young lady.

As part of the adoption agreement, Edna stayed and lived at Everly Hall for as long as she wanted to in exchange for her doing routine chores.

Oakley knew her only as an employee who worked for her parents. Edna was able to watch her grow up and be in her life - even if it was just indirectly.

The Everly Foundation continued to grow, and more and more girls benefited from their generosity.

Not only did unwed mothers come and go but the Everlys opened their doors to troubled girls from all walks of life.

Eventually, the couple hired teachers to tutor them, so they wouldn't fall behind in school. The girls were also taught life skills in a loving environment and left with a feeling of accomplishment and dignity.

In the meantime, Oakley often attended charity events with her parents. During a Christmas Charity Ball, and on a snowy night in December of 1966, a winter storm hit Boston and the surrounding towns.

The storm made driving in the mountains nearly impossible due to low visibility and icy roads. Francis drove around a corner and slid into an oncoming car swerving into his lane.

The two cars hit head on. Everyone was killed instantly.

The news devastated Edna.

Her whole world was taken from her all at once. She hadn't seen or heard from her parents since the day she left them nearly 16 years before.

The attorney's office, "Campbell, Tierney and Waters," contacted her telling her she was listed in the will as the sole heir of the Everly Foundation and Everly Hall School for Girls.

Edna was stunned. Even at 32 years old, she knew nothing about running a business, especially a charity foundation.

The only life she had ever known was working for the Everlys.

Oh, how she missed them!

Edna researched how to make the most of the foundation and went to work on continuing the great legacy left behind by Georgia and Francis Everly.

Laramie

Chapter 4: I am Laramie

The new Eagles' song "Hotel California" gently poured throughout our family's new car.

The rich, new car smell enveloped the space around me. I dozed off for a minute, trying to erase the events that had brought me here.

"Hotel California's" lyrics resonated with us as we drove along the dark highway.

My dad had just brought the new car home to surprise us a few nights before. It was a 1976 Buick Century Wagon with a third-row seat. We were thrilled because now we each had our own row – no more fighting over a seat.

The police car pulling into our driveway quickly put the brakes on all that excitement.

My face turned white as the officer climbed out of his car.

"Mr. Johnson?" he said, in a mild but firm voice.

My father looked at him with concern.

"Yes," he replied. "What can I do for you?"

The officer glanced around at our terrified faces. As if he knew, his eyes rested on me.

"I'm here to arrest your daughter for shoplifting, sir," the officer said.

My older brother, Cody, quickly reached to grab my mother as she fell to the ground in shock.

My world suddenly spun out of control while I stood frozen in my tracks.

Earlier that day, I had been shopping with some friends at the mall. They all had money to buy whatever they wanted, but since my baby sister was born, I hadn't bothered asking my parents for extra cash. They probably would have given it to me, but baby Cheyanne took up all of their time, energy and money lately.

I had become an inconvenience to them – at least that's how it felt to me.

My friends started teasing me when they noticed I wasn't buying anything.

"I'll show them," I thought.

I quickly snuck some earrings into my pocket.

I couldn't believe how easy it was to do so. No one even saw me, and we quietly left the store. My friends all thought I was pretty cool for pulling it off.

As we did more shopping, the challenge continued. Each time I stole something bigger than the last thing I took.

First it was the earrings, then I grabbed a baseball cap.

Next was a purse, then a T-shirt, and finally a pair of jeans. Somehow, I managed to stuff the jeans into one of my friend's bags from another store.

I was getting good at this but figured I had pushed my luck far enough. I had my friends take me home where I tiptoed to my room and quickly hid all my loot under my bed. By the time mom called us to dinner, I had almost forgotten about the whole thing.

As the officer approached me with the handcuffs, my father quickly stepped between the two of us. Dad looked me in the eye.

"What is he talking about, Laramie?" he asked.

With tears streaming down my face, I related the events of the day. Here I was, a straight 'A' student and captain of the high school volleyball team, being arrested in my own front yard!

With shocked looks on their faces, the neighbors stood on their lawns staring across the street - at me.

The officer explained there would need to be special accommodations made for me because I was a minor. They would take me to the station and make arrangements there.

My father convinced them that I was not a flight risk and would not hurt anyone if they wouldn't handcuff me.

The officer looked at my dad and nodded.

Fear and anxiety washed over me as I rubbed my wrists in relief.

The officer read me my rights and placed me in the police car. My parents quickly climbed into the new car and left Cheyanne home with Cody.

Once at the station, they started asking me all kinds of questions.

Question after question.

Police officers' faces just inches from my own.

My heart pounded, and I couldn't breathe.

"Was this your first-time shoplifting?" one officer asked as he moved closer and closer to my face, a cigarette smell wafting from him to me.

"What made you do it?" another demanded.

"Did any of the other girls steal anything?" a third officer asked, his voice rising after he slowly said each word.

My head was spinning. My heart pounded. I felt like throwing up.

I asked my mom for a migraine pill that she always carried with her.

I took the pill and gulped it down thanks to a glass of water an officer handed me. I shut my eyes to block out the searing bright lights. I just needed the world to stop. I needed the noise to stop.

"Stop!" I yelled.

It was really late, so a judge wasn't available to see me. Instead, the jailers assigned a lady officer to stay with me throughout the night ensuring my safety.

I followed her to a holding cell where they had me change my clothes into well-worn and very ugly prison clothes. I felt so cold and dirty.

I wanted to run. I wanted to hide.

Get me out of here! I silently screamed. What had I done?

My mother sobbed as she turned and walked away. I wanted so badly to hug her and tell her it was going to be okay. But I didn't know that it would be.

I laid my head on the rock-hard pillow and cardboard mattress. I tried to sleep but couldn't.

The lady in blue sat down in a chair across from me and read a dog-eared book.

It was going to be a long night for both of us.

I tossed and turned all night. I dreamt someone threw something on my bed. When I woke up, I saw my mom standing there with clean clothes for me to wear.

I showered and scrubbed and scrubbed until my skin bled. It didn't help. I still felt filthy.

Dressed in my clean clothes, I went before the judge. Everyone heard the charges leveled against me. I so badly wanted to run and hide.

"How do you plead to the charges you have been given?" the judge asked.

The Black lady judge was in her mid-forties with a nice face and calm voice. Normally, I may have liked her.

Her hair was pulled back into a ponytail, her makeup neatly applied. She stared at me awaiting my response. I looked at my attorney for some guidance. He nodded and nudged me to respond.

"Guilty, ma'am," I said through tears.

I was lost in all the grownup stuff going on around me.

As decisions were made for me, I watched the disappointment creep across my parents' faces.

It was finally decided that since this was my first offense as a juvenile, I would not be sentenced to prison time.

Relief washed over me, and it all sounded good until the judge started talking again.

"Laramie Johnson, you have been charged with shoplifting multiple items with an estimated value of $500," she said. "It is below the state's $1,000 limit to qualify as a felony, but as a court we agree that you need to be punished for your crime. Therefore, you will serve six months in a home for teen girls. There you will be expected to follow the rules and perform daily acts of service and chores that in time will pay off your debts. Do you understand, Miss Johnson?"

I slowly nodded my head and wiped away the tears streaming down my face. The judge raised her voice slightly.

"Please state your response to the court, Miss Johnson," she calmly said.

"Yes, ma'am." I replied.

The next few days were a blur as arrangements were made for my departure. The judge allowed me to return home with my parents but ordered a tracking device to be placed around my ankle. I felt like an animal being chained up in a cage.

I wasn't allowed to see or talk to my friends. But with friends like these. . . I mused. What kind of friends would encourage someone to steal?

I went through the motions of packing my bags and saying my goodbyes. My mother held me so tight I thought I might break. We both had tears running down our cheeks, but no words were spoken.

I gave Cheyanne a big squeeze. Being just six months old, she had no idea what was going on. Her big blue eyes stared at me in wonder. My older brother wasn't sure what to say or do. I threw my arms around him and sobbed. He hugged me in return and quickly walked away.

The new car, meant to be a way of turning over a new leaf in our family, was now instead taking me to a far-off place we knew nothing about.

My body shook as we drove out of the driveway. We traveled for hours with no words being spoken.

I was terrified. I couldn't sleep.

"I'm sorry, daddy," I whispered.

He didn't respond right away but when he did, his words were thoughtful.

"Your mother and I love you very much. Nothing will ever change that. I am sorry that you have felt neglected lately. It has not been our intent," he said. "I don't want to say anything more now. In a few months after we have all had time apart, we will be reunited and start fresh."

The silence returned.

Only the music from the radio could be heard. The lyrics connected with our surroundings. I raised my head just in time to see a porch light over a freshly painted placard reading, "Everly Hall School for Girls."

Afton

Chapter 5: Meet Afton

Afton quickly splashed cold water on her face hoping to mask the red blotches on her cheeks. The water soothed her and helped her relax from the rigorous workout she had just put her body through.

Afton looked in the mirror and gasped. How would she explain her hair?

Afton's long, blonde hair had fallen into the toilet. She ran her tresses under the water and attempted to dry it with a paper towel.

She glanced in the mirror and moved her shoulders back and forth as she checked out her appearance.

"Not bad," Afton smirked.

She looked somewhat presentable, she thought.

All eyes were on her as she strolled toward the elegantly dressed table.

"Are you feeling alright, Afton?" her mother, Vivian, asked. "You look a bit flushed. Come here and let me check for a fever."

Afton walked slowly toward her mother, who had just finished eating her molten lava chocolate cake.

Wiping her hands with the white linen napkin, Vivian placed the back of her hand on Afton's forehead.

"You don't feel warm," Vivian said. "But let's get you home to bed. You may be coming down with something."

Relieved that no one suspected anything, Afton turned to get her coat from the attendant behind the counter. Afton's father, Charles, gently placed his hand on her back and led her to the round-a-bout to wait for the valet to bring their car around.

Vivian followed close behind and waved to the other guests in their party.

"Let's do this again soon. Have a good evening," she said.

The shiny, black Mercedes pulled forward and the handsome valet climbed out of the car. He gave a quick glance in Afton's direction and politely motioned to her father to get in. The gesture did not go unnoticed, and she shyly smiled back at him.

As the family drove away, Afton checked out the rear window to see him waving goodbye.

The Country Club was about 30 minutes from their home; just long enough for Afton to doze off. Her parents quietly discussed the events of the evening and commented on what a good time they had had with the Carltons.

The Carltons were a new family who had recently moved into the area and joined the Country Club. Since they had a daughter, Cerena, the same age as Afton, they thought it would be fun to get acquainted with them.

As it turned out, the girls didn't have much in common and hadn't hit it off at dinner. Afton seemed to be off in her own world. Once her plate was empty, she quickly excused herself and went to the restroom. Shortly after, Cerena left the table to join Afton.

As Cerena arrived in the restroom, she heard sobbing from inside the stall. Cerena hadn't spoken to Afton all night, and she didn't dare ask Afton if she was alright.

Cerena quietly left the restroom and returned to the table and said that Afton would return shortly.

As soon as Afton returned to the table, her family excused themselves and went home. Once there, Afton went straight to her room. She had a private bathroom and immediately started the shower's hot water.

Exhausted from the evening out, she slowly undressed and climbed into the shower. She let the water run over her face and onto her neck and her shoulders. The steam from the hot water enveloped her increasingly slender body. She noticed that her collar bone protruded more than normal.

Looking down, she saw her exposed ribs and her hip bones sticking out like blades erupting from her skin.

"Success!" she whispered to herself.

Barely able to get out of the shower, Afton gently patted herself dry and placed her feet on the scales. The numbers slowly climbed until stopping at 98 pounds. Last week she weighed 103 pounds. Her plan had worked. She was below 100 pounds.

"Afton," Vivian called from down the hallway. "How are you feeling? Did the shower help? Can I come in?"

Vivian's words echoed in Afton's head making her dizzy.

"I'm feeling much better, mom, thank you," Afton said. "I think I'll just go to bed. Maybe something I ate didn't agree with me."

"Alright then, if you need anything let me know," Vivian said. "Good night, sweetheart."

"Goodnight, mother," Afton said, as she put on her silk nightie.

Afton's nightie slipped off her shoulders reminding her of how much weight she had lost. Feeling drained, she climbed into bed and quickly fell asleep.

The rest of the weekend went by as usual. Afton and her mother played tennis at the club on Saturday morning and had a light brunch following their match.

Afton ate little and didn't purge. But following dinner that night, Afton felt so heavy and so very bloated. She excused herself and rushed to the bathroom.

Everything she had eaten came right back up causing her cheeks to burn. She felt bags forming under eyes.

When Afton came out of the bathroom, Vivian gasped.

"Afton, my goodness, what is wrong with you?" her concerned mother asked.

"I'm fine, mom," Afton said. "Just tired, I think I'll turn in early tonight."

"Don't you have plans with your friends tonight?" Vivian asked.

Afton was supposed to go to the premiere of the new movie, "King Kong." It starred the handsome Jeff Bridges and the beautiful Jessica Lang. She and her friends had spent all week looking forward to opening night.

They had even bought their tickets ahead of time to make sure they had good seats.

The new theater had surround sound. It was going to be a great night. Most of the kids from school were meeting at the movie theater early to get popcorn and other goodies from the snack bar, so they wouldn't miss much of the movie.

"Well, I guess I'll take a short nap before Lilly comes to pick me up," Afton said as she returned to her room.

She collapsed onto her bed and wondered where she would get the strength to go out with friends for the night. Afton's eyes closed, and she fell into a deep sleep.

An hour later, a loud knocking on her door woke Afton up.

"Afton, honey, Lilly is here for you. Are you up to going?" Vivian asked.

Afton quickly jumped from her bed and hit her knee on the nightstand. She winced and gently rubbed her now red and bruised knee.

"I'm coming," she said.

Afton mumbled several colorful words under her breath as she yanked up her now much-too-big jeans and oversized sweater.

She ran a brush through her hair and put it up into a ponytail. A little lip gloss, and she was ready to go.

The theater was loud and full of people. The whole school had turned up for the latest blockbuster.

Afton and her friends, carrying their snacks, stumbled through the dark rows to find their seats. Someone put their foot out as Afton was walking past and caused her to spill her popcorn on the floor.

"What do you think you're doing?" Afton yelled.

The girls in the row began to giggle and mocked Afton as she fumbled to get to her chair. Finally in her seat, she managed to get comfortable as the previews started.

Afton suddenly heard cheers and clapping announcing the end of the movie. She had slept through the whole thing!

"Well, what did you think of it?" Lilly looked over at her and asked.

"It was really good, huh?" Afton replied.

The ride home was full of chit chat as everyone rehashed the events of the movie. Afton played along as well as she could.

She was relieved when she was the first to be dropped off.

"See you Monday!" Afton said as she climbed out of the car.

Afton rushed into the house and went directly to her room.

Her parents had told her not to wake them when she got home.

They knew it would be after midnight, and they trusted her to come straight home.

Afton was relieved not to discuss the movie with them.

Sunday morning came, and Afton spent the entire day in bed. Since her mother thought Afton was coming down with something, it wouldn't seem strange for Afton to be sleeping.

Afton managed to get out of bed to use the bathroom. At some point last night, she gulped down the root beer she purchased.

Seeing the scales, Afton stepped on them. She slowly opened her eyes to see the number at 96.

Rubbing her eyes to be sure, she looked again.

"Maybe this is getting out of control," she thought to herself as she climbed back into bed and pulled the blankets over her head.

Monday morning came bright and early. Afton gradually made her way out of bed and into the shower. She gazed down at her skeleton of a body.

In her mind Afton still saw herself as overweight but could not deny the numbers staring at her from the bathroom scales. She quickly got dressed and ran down the stairs for breakfast.

Vivian had prepared waffles with fresh strawberries and whipped cream. Afton knew if she ate them, she would risk gaining back the weight she had recently lost.

"You need your strength, Afton," her mother said.

Afton put a small waffle on her plate as her mother smothered it with strawberries and whipped topping.

Nausea washed over Afton as she looked at the food.

She didn't want to draw attention to herself.

Appearances meant everything to her father. He was a partner at the prestigious law firm of Campbell, Tierney and Waters in downtown Boston. She couldn't risk embarrassing him.

After cleaning her plate, Afton excused herself and ran to the bathroom. Shortly after, Lilly picked her up.

Once inside the car, Afton was surprised to see Cerena Carlton sitting in the front seat next to Lilly. That is where Afton usually sat, so they could discuss the weekend.

Afton timidly climbed into the back seat next to Lilly's annoying younger brother, Brody.

Cerena started talking about the dinner at the Country Club and didn't hesitate to mention that Afton left the table in a hurry.

Cerena went on and on about how she had followed Afton into the bathroom and heard Afton crying. Cerena continued to elaborate about how Afton returned to dinner looking flushed.

Brody looked at Afton and saw something in her hair. He tried to be sneaky about letting her know, but Lilly was watching in the rearview mirror.

"What is going on with you, Afton?" she said sharply.

"First, you fall asleep in the movie, and now I hear this!" Lilly said. "I knew something was up. All your clothes are falling off of you, and you look awful."

Tears streamed down both Afton's and Lilly's cheeks as Lilly pulled the car over to the curb.

"We're going to be late for school," Cerena whined.

"Then get out and walk," Lilly replied.

Lilly grabbed some tissues out of the glove compartment and walked around to the back seat. She opened the door and embraced Afton.

"We're going to get you some help," she whispered softly in her ear.

The two held each other for several minutes before anyone spoke.

Cerena broke the silence.

"Hop in, Lilly," she said. "I'll drive you both back home. Then I'll get me and Brody to school. We'll just have to be late. Some things are more important."

Shocked, Lilly slid into the back seat next to Afton. Brody sat quietly and watched what was happening.

Cerena pulled the car forward into traffic and drove to the Campbell residence. Afton and Lilly got out of the car and slowly walked to the front door. Noticing the car in the driveway, Vivian ran to meet them.

"What's wrong, Lilly?" she cried as they all went inside.

"Afton needs help," Lilly said.

Vivian reached for her phone and called her husband.

Mr. Campbell remembered a client, Ms. Edna King, who ran the Everly Hall School for girls. He had heard great things about the Everly Foundation, and the good things it did for troubled teenagers.

Mr. and Mrs. Everly, the founders, passed away several years ago, but the school continued to be a respected facility by the community. It was a place he felt comfortable sending his daughter. He would call and see if he could get her in right away.

That was the first step to a long road of recovery.

Eevie

Chapter 6: Meet Eevie

"Good night, sleep tight. Don't let the bed bugs bite!"

The familiar phrase echoed in Eevie's ears as she laid her head on the clean, flower-covered pillowcase.

It was the first night in a new house, and she couldn't sleep. Although the bed was warm and cozy, she didn't feel comfortable enough to snuggle in and relax.

The events of the previous days kept running through her mind. Coming home from school, she had seen lots of cars she didn't recognize in the driveway. That usually meant that mom had "friends" over.

Eevie never liked it when strangers were there after school. She would be told to go to her room and shut the door. Wanting a snack from the kitchen was forbidden, so she would do her homework while listening to her stomach growl.

That day was different.

Instead of being sent to her room, one of the guys asked her if she wanted to join them.

Eevie looked around the room to find her mother's face. When she couldn't see it, she started to yell for her.

Quickly, the man placed his hand over her mouth and told her to be quiet. Her mother, Colleen, ran into the living room screaming at him to let Eevie go. Instead, he laughed and held her tighter.

Eevie squirmed and struggled for breath. The others in the room told the man to let her go as she fell lifeless to the ground.

Colleen gasped and dropped to Eevie's side. Colleen checked for her daughter's pulse.

"She's alive!" Colleen shouted.

While Eevie was alive, she wasn't responding.

Just as Colleen called out for someone to dial 911, an explosion muffled her cries.

Darkness filled the entire house, and smoke consumed them. Eevie's mother grabbed a hold of her sleeve and pulled Eevie outside onto the porch. Coughing and trying to catch her breath, Colleen looked around at the bodies scattered across the front yard. It seemed as if everything was moving in slow motion.

Exhausted, Colleen collapsed.

The sounds of sirens and flashing lights woke Eevie up. Unsure of what had happened, Eevie sat up and saw her mother lying next to her.

"Mommy, wake up! Wake up!" Eevie cried as she shook Colleen.

Colleen opened her eyes and stared blankly up at her daughter's face. Eevie reached up to wipe the tears from her own ash covered cheeks. Time stood still as they sat motionless on the concrete.

Suddenly, an officer approached them.

"Are you alright?" he asked.

His deep voice shocked Colleen.

"I think so. What happened?" she replied.

The police officer explained that the house had gone up in flames. The reason was still unclear, and it was under investigation. He told them that there were multiple fatalities, and several others who were injured.

"You are both very lucky," he said. "Let's get you over to the medic and get you checked out."

Slowly, the officer helped them both to their feet. Weak from the smoke in her lungs, Colleen nearly fell back down as she struggled to stand.

"Can I get some help over here?" the officer yelled out.

Quickly a young, female officer came running towards them. She took Eevie and carefully helped her walk to the ambulance. Colleen followed behind with the other officer's arm around her for support.

The ambulance served as a respite from the chaos going on around them.

The paramedic listened to their lungs and placed oxygen masks on each of them to assist with their breathing. One of the medical assistants used a cool, damp cloth to carefully wash the black soot from their faces.

Eevie cried out in pain, not realizing that her eyebrows had been singed from the fire. Her hands had been burned as well.

"It hurts," Colleen said as she gently rubbed her injured hands.

The burns needed to be taken care of at the hospital. The ambulance doors were shut tight as the ambulance pulled out into the road towards the Littleton Medical Center.

"What have I done?" Colleen mumbled under her breath as her daughter wrestled in her sleep on the cot across from her.

Eevie and Colleen stayed in the hospital for a couple of days for burn care and observation.

The fire marshal discovered that the home had been a meth house. Left unattended, the hazardous chemicals got so hot that it burst into flames and exploded.

Some of the people inside couldn't escape in time and succumbed to the blaze. Fortunately, Eevie and her mother had been close to the front door and had gotten out.

After extensive questioning, the police learned it was Colleen's home. Officers learned that Colleen had assisted in meth production for several months.

Since Eevie was only 15 and a minor, she needed to be placed in the custody of Child Protective Services. Colleen faced jail time for running a meth lab and involuntary manslaughter for the deaths of three people.

A nice lady in her 50's came to the hospital room and introduced herself as Mrs. Redmond from the Health and Welfare office. She informed Eevie that she would be taking her to live temporarily with a foster family.

This wasn't the first time Eevie had heard these words.

Years ago, police arrested her mother for drug possession. Colleen had gotten clean and had Eevie returned to her. Now, the chances of that happening again were slim to none.

Eevie watched in silence as they put her mother in handcuffs and took her away.
The thoughts slowly faded, and Eevie fell asleep. For the first time in several days, she slept soundly.

Eevie dreamt of swimming in a cool pond with a majestic waterfall, the beautiful blue sky overhead. She couldn't remember a time when she felt more safe and more relaxed.

Hours later, the sound of small children running down the hallway woke up Eevie and brought her back to reality, reminding her of where she really was.

After making the bed, Eevie put on the bathrobe neatly folded on the footstool. It smelled fresh as if it had just been washed.

Eevie couldn't recall ever wearing a clean smelling piece of clothing. Her clothes always had the lingering odor of ammonia or rotten eggs. The clean clothes felt so good as she put on the shirt and pants.

Eevie noticed an empty bed next to hers that she hadn't seen the night before. She took a deep breath and opened the door to meet her new "family."

The aroma of bacon and eggs filled the kitchen.

Everyone huddled around the kitchen table waiting for their plate to be filled. Suddenly the commotion came to an abrupt stop as all faces turned to look at Eevie, who was now the new girl. Eevie could feel her cheeks turning red as they all stared at her.

"Good morning," Eevie said.

Sharon, the foster mother, turned from the stove to greet her.

"And good morning to you," Sharon said. "Children, please welcome Eevie. She will be joining us for a while."

She motioned for Eevie to take a seat and placed a plate of food in front of her.

Hesitating, she picked up a fork and took a bite. The food was delicious, and Eevie continued eating until she realized all eyes were on her.

"We haven't had the bwessing yet," a curly haired little girl quietly said,

Eevie froze with her mouth full of scrambled eggs.

"Oh, I'm sorry," she mumbled. She quickly swallowed her food and folded her arms.

"It's yo tuin," the little girl said.

Eevie looked at Sharon for approval, and she nodded in response.

Eevie had never said a prayer before, so she asked the little girl for help.

"Thank you God fo this food and fo a place to wiv," the little girl whispered. "Pwease bwess Momma Shawan and all the childwen. And bwess the food. Amen."

Eevie's eyes burned as they filled with tears.

She reached for a napkin to wipe them away before anyone noticed.

With the blessing said, the children returned to their plates and finished their breakfast. Eevie watched as they visited with each other and then carried their dishes to the sink.

There were six children in all, including Eevie. Four boys and now two girls. Each one dressed in clean clothes with their hair neatly combed.

The little girl with curly, blonde hair climbed onto Eevie's lap.

"My name is Sawa and I am fo yees od," Sawa said.

Sharon interrupted her.

"This is Sara, and she is four years old. She is excited to have another girl in the house." Sharon said. "I hope you don't mind sharing a room with her. We are a bit crowded right now."

"That explains the other bed," Eevie whispered to herself. "No, I don't mind at all. It will be fun."

The following days were busy getting settled in. Just as Eevie was getting comfortable in her new surroundings, she learned she would move into a home for teen girls. Her bed was needed for a new placement, and since Eevie was a teenager, she was the one who would be moved.

Sara was sad until she learned that there would be another little girl moving in. Eevie was excited for her to have someone to play with but wary of what was ahead for herself.

Eevie was told that Everly Hall School for Girls had a reputation of being strict, but not harsh. Education and life lessons were taught in a firm but loving environment.

It opened as a home for unwed mothers but had evolved into a safe place for girls in varying situations such as temporary housing, trouble with the law and mental or medical issues.

Colleen still had several months of rehab to complete and wouldn't be able to see Eevie until her classes were finished. She was also serving jail time and had nowhere for them to live once she was released.

Her court date had not yet been set for the impending involuntary manslaughter charges. The future was unclear, but one thing was certain; Eevie was starting a new chapter in her life.

Kyla

Chapter 7: Meet Kyla

Prom was the most highly anticipated event at Freeport High.

Kyla Armstrong was Jr. Class President, and it was one of her duties to plan the Jr./Sr. Prom.

She had been planning for months.

Kyla finally confirmed her reservation at the Sugarbush Farms venue. The caterers had finalized the menu. The junior class had raised enough money to ensure the best prom ever held in Freeport.

Fundraising began last summer with a kick-off carwash and bake sale. The entire town had shown up to support the local high school students. It was a hot July day, and the sun was beating down on them. The only reprieve was the cold water coming from the hoses.

One accidental spray and the fight was on!

Wet, soapy towels swung carelessly around the parking lot. Cars and their drivers were caught in the onslaught of sun-burned teens and out-of-control water hoses.

As Kyla turned around, a dirty, ragged dish towel slapped her across her face. She just about said something colorful when she realized that a handsome young man was the culprit.

Just steps away, Kyla looked into the bluest eyes she had ever seen. His light curls were damp and mussed up but still fell perfectly into place. She stood in shock as he reached for a dry towel.

"I am so sorry," he managed to say as he tripped over his tongue. "I didn't mean to hit you in the face."

Mr. Blue Eyes handed her the clean towel.

"My name is Preston Rhodes. I just moved here last week," he said.

"Nice… to … meet…you," Kyla stammered as she quickly turned and ran away.

The following day, there was a knock on Kyla's front door. When she answered it, there stood Preston Rhodes in all his glory. With his perfectly groomed hair and warm smile, Kyla was instantly smitten.

"Hello," she said. "What can I do for you?"

"Well, for starters, you could tell me where to get a good burger and fries around here," he said. "Then you could join me for some lunch," he replied.

Kyla was surprised by his suggestion but excused herself to get a sweater.

"I believe I can do both, Mr. Rhodes. Let's go!" she said.

Closing the door behind her, Kyla followed him to his blue 1970 Chevelle. The color matched his eyes, and she found herself awestruck.

He opened the car door for her, and she slid in. Preston walked around to his side of the car.

"Where to?" he asked as Kyla pointed the way to the Frosty Palace.

The car hop took their order of two cheeseburgers, an order of fries and a chocolate shake to share.

"We should probably get to know each other better if you intend for me to be your girlfriend," Kyla said.

"Don't you think that's a bit presumptuous of you, Miss Armstrong?" he responded.

Kyla giggled while Preston pulled her in close to him. Just then the food arrived, and they put the two straws into the milkshake.

They took a sip together while staring into each another's eyes. From that day on, they were inseparable, except when they said a reluctant good night.

The summer brought drive-in movies, bonfires and Saturday night dances. Soon the temperatures started to drop, and it was time to go back to school.

Pep rallies and football games filled the weekends. Preston was made quarterback, and Kyla never missed a game.

Although she wasn't the cheerleader type, Kyla yelled just as loudly from the stands. Student Council was more her style, and she encouraged school spirit as part of her platform. Students supported her efforts, and their cheering section always yelled louder than the opposing teams.

Throughout the school year, Kyla and Preston maintained their relationship. Preston was a senior and had started thinking about his future. He had been accepted at a university and received a football scholarship.

With Kyla having another year of high school, she assumed Preston would move on without her. But Preston had other ideas. He wanted to stay together and pursue a long-distance relationship. Kyla wasn't sure that's what she wanted. She had enjoyed their fun times together, but never assumed it would last forever.

Kyla and her girlfriends went shopping and bought the perfect prom dresses. Hers was yellow with tiny white roses scattered about the bodice, and a full skirt was gathered in at the waist with a satin ribbon. She looked like Cinderella going to the ball.

Preston rented a pale blue tux to bring out his eyes and would pair it with a yellow tie to match Kyla's dress.

He ordered Kyla a corsage with baby yellow roses and white baby's breath for her. The flower shop added a white single rose boutonniere for Preston. They would be the best-looking couple at the prom.

The morning of the dance finally arrived.

The Student Council was in charge of the decorations. Kyla arrived early to give herself time to get ready after setting up at the venue.

She delegated several individuals to oversee certain areas of the space. She felt confident in her assignments, but looking around, she noticed that one of the boys was not there. He was in charge of the stage for the band. If it wasn't done correctly, the band couldn't perform.

Kyla began to panic, just as her old boyfriend Jordan came running in out of breath. They had grown up together, and he still had feelings for her.

Jordan tried to hide those feelings but failed. The entire student body knew he still liked her. Afterall, they had all known each other since kindergarten.

Preston was the new kid in town, and they never let him forget it.

Relieved, Kyla ran to Jordan's side.

"Where have you been?" she demanded. "The band will be here any minute to set up."

"So sorry, Kyla. I had an errand to run," he said. "I promise you it will be ready for them. I won't let you down."

Jordan started to walk away as he felt Kyla's hand on his arm.

"I know you won't. You never have," she said.

Everyone frantically moved about the venue preparing for the big night. By one o'clock, they were satisfied with the results.

"See you tonight!" Kyla yelled to her friends as she reached to turn off the lights.

Taking one final glance of approval, she flipped the switch and locked the doors.

The afternoon was spent at the beauty salon getting a mani/pedi and an updo to Kyla's hair.

Preston was picking her up at six o'clock for dinner at the fanciest steakhouse in town. They were meeting two other couples there and would then follow each other to Sugarbush Farms for the dance.

When six o'clock rolled around, Preston honked for Kyla. Her father would not stand for that.

"What kind of boy is he that honks for my daughter?" her dad demanded. "He can come to the door and properly pick you up."

Kyla stood embarrassed as she waited. Getting the idea, Preston got out of his car and sheepishly walked up the sidewalk to the front door. He raised his hand and knocked three times.

Mr. Armstrong opened the door and invited him in. Kyla stood waiting patiently to be addressed by either of them. Eventually her mother broke the silence and suggested they take some pictures.

Preston rolled his eyes, moved close to Kyla and posed for the camera. The Polaroid instantly produced photos for them to preview.

"Where are the flowers?" her mother asked.

Preston quickly ran out to his car to retrieve them. When he returned, he awkwardly placed the corsage on Kyla's chest as the flash went off on the camera once again.

He stood still while Kyla attempted to pin the boutonniere on his jacket. Finally, Mrs. Armstrong offered to help. This time it was Kyla who took the picture.

Flowers in place and photos completed, the two walked to the car. Preston realized her father was watching and made sure to open the door for Kyla. Once settled, they drove toward the restaurant.

The other couples were waiting inside and motioned for them to join them at the reserved table. The girls greeted each other and commented on how beautiful they each looked.

The guys shook hands and argued over who's date was the hottest.

The waitress came to take their drink order. Preston joked that he was of age and tried to order alcohol. The waitress was not amused and threatened to get the manager.

Kyla placed her hand on his knee and gave him the look that said, "What are you trying to prove?" He quickly ordered a soft drink and started a new conversation.

"What's everyone going to have?" Preston asked.

Steak and seafood dinners were served, and they finished that off with some Key Lime Pie for dessert.

"So, we'll see you at the dance." Preston said, as he put his hand on Kyla's back to hurry her along.

"What's the rush, Preston? The dance doesn't start for 30 minutes," she said.

"Well, don't you need to be there early to check on the band?" he replied.

"I guess that wouldn't be a bad idea," she agreed.

Preston escorted Kyla to the car, and they drove away.

Two hours later, Kyla's friends started worrying about her. No one had seen either her or Preston at the dance. It was time to announce Prom King and Prom Queen.

Kyla and Preston were the favored couple according to dance gossip. Just as the emcee was about to open the envelope, Kyla and Preston entered the building.

All eyes were on the couple.

"And the titles of Prom King and Queen go to Preston Rhodes and Kyla Armstrong!" the emcee announced.

Everyone cheered as they made their way to the front of the crowd. Preston gloated in his glory, and Kyla shyly accepted the crown and sash being placed over her shoulder.

Jordan looked on from the back of the room and noticed mascara running down Kyla's cheeks. One could assume she was emotional over the win, but Jordan knew her better than that.

Prom came to an end, and the cleanup committee was left in charge. Luckily, the Student Council had fulfilled its assignment and could go home.

Kyla thanked the band, and everyone else who had helped her pull off the successful event. If only she herself could have enjoyed it more.

Preston pulled into the driveway and practically pushed Kyla out of the car.

"Aren't you going to walk me to the door?" she asked, confused.

"You got your crown and the perfect prom; you don't need me anymore." Preston gruffly replied.

Stunned, Kyla grasped the car door handle and paused briefly.

"What do you mean?" she asked.

"Just get out of the car!" he yelled.

Kyla had barely climbed out as Preston sped away into the darkness.

Two months later, Preston and the rest of the class of 1976 graduated from Freeport High. Things had been different since prom, and the two had hardly even spoken to each other. Kyla tried to forget what had happened that night.

She knew he would be off to college soon on his football scholarship and would never look back.

Kyla, however, would have a constant reminder of her Jr. Prom.

Summer came, and with it came bikini season.

The kids from school were planning a day at the beach to celebrate the beginning of their senior year of high school.

Kyla had successfully hidden her baby bump until now.

How could she keep her secret any longer?

She considered making up an excuse for not going, but really didn't want to miss out on the fun.

It was time to come clean. Decisions needed to be made, and her parents needed to know.

The night before the beach party, Kyla told her parents she needed to talk to them about something. After the dinner dishes had been put away, they met in the living room.

With tears in her eyes, she replayed the events of prom night to her mother and father.

Resisting the urge to say something he knew he would regret, Mr. Armstrong put his arms around his daughter and wept. Mrs. Armstrong sat in silence as the news sunk in.

Kyla was pregnant.

Arrangements were made for Kyla to attend her senior year of high school at Everly Hall School for Girls.

In addition to food and accommodations, she would receive counseling services and guidance in a loving atmosphere. Living with other girls in similar circumstances would hopefully alleviate any type of judgment or gossip.

Over the coming months, she could decide what she would do with the baby. She knew she wanted to carry the baby but wasn't sure about what to do after it was born.

Preston didn't even know, and she wanted it that way for as long as possible.

Without saying goodbye to her friends, Kyla disappeared one hot, summer day.

It had been exactly one year since the carwash that started it all.

Chapter 8: Arrival Day: Part One

The sun was just beginning to rise as we pulled into the parking lot of the Everly Hall School for Girls.

We drove all night, and we were both exhausted.

Slowly, dad got out of the car and stretched his arms high above his head. He took a deep breath as he struggled to stand up.

I sat quietly in the back seat and stared out the window. Nestled in the trees at the end of the dirt road was a large wooden building with a freshly painted "Welcome" sign hanging on the front porch.

"Oh, how cozy," I mumbled to myself.

Scooting to the end of the bench row where I had been sleeping, I opened the car door. The air was clean, and I could hear birds chirping overhead as if saying "hello" - quite a contrast from the noise and smells of downtown Boston that I was used to.

"Rise and shine, Laramie, sweetheart," I heard my father's voice encouraging me. "It's time to get on with it."

I forced myself out of the car and grabbed my sweater from off the seat. Although it was July, the morning air was chilly in the mountains. I slipped my arms into my sweater and felt a piece of home wrapped around me. Picking up the suitcases, my dad and I walked up the gravel path leading to the front door. I noticed the other girls and their families making the same long, awkward walk.

Obviously, no one was eager to be first in line.

The Everly Hall School for Girls was built in 1950 by a man named Francis Everly. He and his wife, Georgia, couldn't have children of their own, so they built the home for unwed mothers needing a place to live.

For several years it served as a refuge for these girls and their babies until they either placed the baby for adoption or were able to be on their own. The Everlys owned the property until their deaths in 1966.

Everly Hall housed up to 40 girls. Each of the 20 rooms had a murphy bed that was shared by two girls. There was a kitchenette with a sink and an apartment size refrigerator. Each room had its own private bathroom. All rooms had two exits - one from the shared hall and a sliding glass door allowing access to the enclosed garden area.

There was also a fire pit for campfires during the cold fall and winter nights.

"I feel like I'm arriving for summer camp," Laramie sighed.

Yet, it wasn't summer camp. It was instead a place for pregnant or troubled young girls to stay until things got better for them.

The confused and scared faces of young girls looked into each other's eyes. All of us were afraid and fearing the unknown.

Suddenly, a tall, well-groomed woman opened the front door and stepped out onto the front porch. Everyone went silent, as if the President of the United States had appeared.

She wore a dark blue suit and pointed black shoes. She appeared to be about 50 years old with soft age lines appearing on her forehead and around her mouth. She cleared her throat loudly.

"Welcome to you all. I hope you will be comfortable here for the duration of your stay, no matter how long that may be," the woman said. "My name is Edna King, and I am in charge here at Everly Hall. You may call me Ms. King. If you could please form an orderly line that would be appreciated. One parent may accompany you through the registration process, and then you will say your good-byes."

Edna rattled off the rules and emphasized that no one other than the girls were allowed in the dorm rooms. She noted that there was an open area for visitation days once a month.

"Your family can visit with you then," she said. "Now then, let's get you all registered."

Everyone quickly moved into a somewhat orderly line and wiggled their way into the front door. Inside were three check-in desks arranged alphabetically: A-I, J-P and Q-Z.

My dad and I made our way to the second desk.

"What is your name, please?" asked a young lady who wore a name tag that said, "Hello, my name is Mary."

"Laramie Johnson," I quietly replied.

"Welcome, Laramie," Mary said. "You will be in room A-3. Your roommate is Kyla Armstrong. Take your bags to your room and get settled in. Say goodbye to your father before going down the hall. You can see him in a few weeks. Lunch is at noon."

I glanced at my father as tears ran down his cheeks. I felt like crying too but held it together for his sake. I had to appear strong, so he could leave me behind to pay for what I had done. It was such a stupid thing, I thought.

I threw my arms around his waist and hugged him tight. He hugged me back. I didn't want him to let go, but eventually he pulled back and looked me in the eyes.

"You've got this. I love you," he said.

And with that, he turned and walked away.

I gathered my belongings and made my way down the steps leading to the dorm rooms. The sign above the archway showed a large letter "A", indicating that I was in the correct hall. I was looking for room A-3 when I heard a voice behind me.

"Hey, wait up!" someone called.

I turned around and saw a girl with dark hair and big brown eyes running after me. The little amount of running that she had done shouldn't have caused someone to be so out of breath, but it soon became apparent why she was panting.

"Slow down. Where's the fire?" I asked as I allowed her to catch up with me.

"Hi, my name is Kyla. I guess we're going to be roommates," she said.

"I'm Laramie," I said and paused for a moment. "Nice to meet you. Shall we find our room then?"

Kayla and I continued down the hall glancing at each room number.

"Here we are, A-3." Kyla stopped in front of the door and placed her bags on the floor.

"Do you want to do the honors?" she said.

I slowly approached the handle and realized the door had been left ajar. I pushed it forward to expose what was to be our new "home."

We each proceeded to unpack our bags and tried to make our space look as much like home as possible. We engaged in small talk with neither of us willing to share much personal information yet. We were just two teenage girls who were forced to live together thanks to undesirable circumstances.

Trust was something that had to be earned.

By noon, all of the new girls had checked in, and it was time for lunch in the main dining hall.

Tension filled the room like a heavy fog as the girls entered. Vulnerable and scared was the best way to describe what we were all feeling.

The current residents stood at one end of the hall waiting to escort the new girls to their assigned tables.

The dining room was bright and airy, surrounded by windows. Five round tables were set up throughout the room giving it more of a home dining room vibe. Colorful tablecloths and a small vase of fresh flowers adorned each of the tables. There were eight chairs at each table with a place setting arranged for proper dining etiquette.

Kyla and I slowly approached the dining room. We looked around and noticed a girl walking towards us. She had a name tag that read "Molly." She handed us two stickers and a black sharpie and instructed us to write our names on them. We each did so and placed the name tags on our blouses.

"Please follow me," Molly said. "I'll show you where you will be sitting for the first month. After that you will be assigned to a new table to get acquainted with different girls. Here we are."

The other six girls were already seated, and all eyes went directly to Kyla's protruding tummy.

"What's wrong with you all? Never seen a pregnant girl before?" Laramie exclaimed as they entered the room.

Chapter 9: Arrival Day: Part Two

Kyla and I took our places in the two remaining seats.

Luckily, they were side by side. We had only known each other for a couple of hours, but she made me feel safe in a room full of total strangers.

I still wasn't sure if we would be friends, but at least she was now a familiar face.

"Hello everyone, my name is Laramie. Just like it says on my name tag." I introduced myself, hoping to break the awkward silence.

"I'm Kyla," she said.

The other girls slowly went around the table telling us their names. Two of the girls, Maggie and Lisa had been living here for the last three months.

Maggie had an anger management issue, and Lisa was just the opposite, being extremely shy. We soon learned that Afton and Eevie were in the room right next door to us in A-5.

Afton was a tall, very thin, blonde-haired beauty. Although she had striking blue eyes, they seemed almost hollow - as if you could see straight through her. She played with her food and showed very little interest in eating it, occasionally taking an obligatory bite.

Next to her sat Eevie. Eevie was one of the most beautiful young women I had ever seen. With her smooth, black skin and dark eyes, she reminded me of a movie star.

She had her dark, curly hair pulled back into a loose bun on top of her head. We all sat quietly wondering what misfortune had brought us all together.

Finally, Ms. King stood to address us.

"Ahem," she began as she tapped a pencil on the lectern.

It seemed she always had to clear her throat before speaking.

"I hope you are all enjoying your lunch today," she said. "Our cooks work especially hard to make good tasting, nutritional meals for you."

A soft groan came from the room. Yet, I found the chicken sandwich and french fries to be quite delightful.

"Please finish up your dessert and return to your rooms for a short nap," Ms. King said. "We will meet at 4 for a get-to-know-you gathering in the game room before dinner."

Just as she sat down, the kitchen staff delivered a cup of vanilla ice cream to each of us. We happily devoured it and returned to our respective rooms for our rest period.

Once in our room, we promptly pulled out the murphy bed. But napping was the last thing on our minds. So many things to talk about. So much to discover about each other.

Obviously, the elephant in the room was the baby bump.

"So, I guess you're wondering what my story is?" Kyla said.

"Only when you're ready to share it." I replied.

With tears in her eyes, Kyla related the events of her prom night. I wasn't exactly sure how to react, so I just listened and reluctantly hugged her. At first it felt a bit awkward, but I could tell she appreciated it. It would be the beginning of many more.

I shared my story about the day at the mall and about my so-called "friends" who encouraged me to steal. I felt tears burning in my own eyes as Kyla reached out to touch my hand.

We had both been deceived by people we trusted.

Laying our heads back on the pillows and snuggled in the blankets, we succumbed to the much-needed rest and fell sound asleep.

A loud knock on the door brought us out of dreamland. I jumped up to answer it and saw Afton and Eevie waiting on the other side.

"Wake up, sleepy heads! It's time to get to know each other," they said practically in unison.

Eevie was a little too cheery for me at the moment, but I was glad for the wake-up call. We quickly brushed through our hair and jogged to the game room as we knew there were consequences for being late.

Upon entering the room, we were handed a paper with questions on it.

We were to go around the room and ask different girls to answer them.

Some of the questions were easy like: "Where do you live?" "What is your name, and how old are you?"

Others were harder to ask such as "What is your greatest fear?" and "What are you scared of?" and "What is your dream?"

It was a fun icebreaker, but when it came to me answering the questions, I found it a little intimidating.

This was personal stuff that I really hadn't given much thought to. I wasn't sure I was prepared to share this information with total strangers. This was going to get deep.

Maybe that's part of the plan, I mused.

After about 30 minutes of the game, Mary announced that it was time to find a seat. The girls scattered to find a chair next to someone they knew.

Kyla and I were fortunate enough to locate two empty chairs side by side. Afton and Eevie were already seated at the same table. Maybe this wouldn't be so bad after all.

Edna King stood to address us, cleared her throat again and tapped a pencil on a lectern.

"As some of you may know, I was the first resident here at Everly Hall. In 1950, a loving couple offered to let me live here during a difficult time of my life," she said as she wiped away a tear. "At the age of 16, I was kicked out of my house because I was pregnant and not married. Mr. and Mrs. Francis Everly gave me a safe place to live and adopted my baby girl. The three of them were killed in a tragic car accident coming home from a charity event. I was written into their will as their only heir. Since that day, I have done my best to keep Everly Hall the safe and loving respite they intended it to be."

Everyone was shocked.

Ms. King wasn't some snooty, old lady trying to make misfortunate young ladies more miserable than they already were. She was, in fact, just like one of the girls she was now helping.

"She's one of us," Laramie thought.

No one said a word while they let the news sink in.

"Now that you know a little bit about me, it is your turn to share with each other what brought you here," Edna said. "Remember that this is a safe place, and no judgements are to be made. Take your time and listen to each story as if it were your own."

Soon a low, steady rumble of soft voices was heard telling heartfelt experiences that shaped who we all were. Quiet tears were shed, and hands were held offering loving support.

Just a few short hours before, we had all been strangers, now we felt like family. Of course, some of us still had trust issues.

The six of us stared at one another for a few minutes.

I decided to break the ice by telling my story. As I shared the events of the day at the mall, it became very evident that those girls had not been my friends at all. They didn't care about me. They only cared about outward appearances and being the best.

Sure, it had been cool to be the captain of the volleyball team, but I worked hard to get there. They only played on the team for the popularity of it. I studied hard to maintain my 4.0 GPA, while they were off partying, and then begged me for the answers to the tests.

I had been such a fool to think they were my friends. Here, at this table I was surrounded by people who seemed to really care about me. Time would tell if that was true.

One by one the others shared their stories. With tears in her eyes, Kyla explained the obvious question on everyone's mind. She still hadn't told the baby's father, Preston, about the baby. She felt ashamed and embarrassed that she fell for his games.

"I trusted him!" Kyla cried.

Kyla held Eevie's hand while she expressed the sorrow she felt over being separated from her mother. She tried holding back the tears while the incident played out in our minds.

Eevie described the horrifying sound of the explosion, and the realization of what happened.

Foster care had been a safe place for her and being here was both a new and frightening experience. Being the only Black girl in the room frightened her even more.

The girls at the table expressed their sincere loyalty to her, and she felt comfort in their words.

Maggie and Lisa had already let us know why they were each living at Everly Hall. Three months ago, they arrived on the same day as total opposites, but were now the best of friends.

Maggie kept getting in fights at both school and at home. When she became violent, her parents sent her to a doctor. He recommended sending her to the Everly Hall School for Girls.

Maggie resisted and refused to go; yet, with the threat of not graduating from high school hanging over her head, she finally agreed to go. A college education and becoming a surgeon were her lifelong dreams. She wasn't about to let anything, or anybody, cause her to lose sight of her goals.

Lisa had been diagnosed with a form of autism that caused her to "freeze" in front of people. She was extremely bright, with an IQ of 133, but she had trouble concentrating.

Because of her inability to focus in a standard classroom, her parents thought it would be a good idea for her to be in a more controlled learning environment. During her three months at Everly Hall, she completed her junior year of high school and planned on returning to public school in the fall.

Listening to her now, you would never know that she had a problem opening up in the past.

Afton was the last to speak up.

We could all tell she struggled in finding the right words. There were candy kisses scattered on the table, and Afton had fidgeted with the wrappers for the last hour. Not once had she put one in her mouth. The chocolate candy turned into a melted mess in her fingers.

"Afton, do you have anything you want to say?" I finally asked.

She looked at me with her shallow eyes and cried.

"I have an eating disorder," she quietly admitted as she cast her eyes down.

No other explanation was needed in that moment as we all lowered our heads and reached for each other's hands under the table. We sat in silent prayer and absorbed all that had just transpired.

Maybe we could all be friends after all.

Time was up, and Ms. King stood to announce that dinner would be served in the dining room in 15 minutes. We slowly stood up from our tables and walked hand in hand to our spaghetti and meatballs.

Chapter 10: Visiting Day

The following days were spent unpacking, getting acquainted, and registering for our fall classes.

Maggie and Lisa prepared to leave by the end of summer, so their schedules were a little different and more laid back. That gave them time to spend with us and helped us feel more at ease with the changes happening in our lives.

After the night of introductions, there had been a sense of respect developed for one another. The unspoken words between us gave me comfort in knowing I had a support system.

I could get through the next six months.

Before we knew it, visiting day was here. A whole month had passed, and normalcy had set in. Our routine included waking up at 6:30 a.m., making our beds, showering and being ready for breakfast at 7:30 a.m.

Fall classes started the following month, but we still had a few weeks to settle in.

The day we were dropped off at the school had been a scary time full of anticipation of the unknown. I couldn't wait to see my family again; yet, now that Visiting Day was here, I felt a new wave of emotions.

Everything had to be perfect for Visiting Day. For most of us, it would be the first time we had seen our family members since we were dropped off.

The girls who had been here for a while were used to being reconnected with their loved ones and were familiar with the events of the day, but for me it was a new and awkward experience.

Thoughts surged through my mind.

I wondered if they would hold my past against me. How would my family treat me? Would things return to normal, or would there be a new normal?

After breakfast, we returned to our rooms to make final preparations for our families' arrivals. I wasn't sure who all would be coming, but I was anxious to see whoever showed up.

I had been so busy that - as much as I hated to admit it - I hadn't had time to miss my family. But now the reality of it all was setting in.

The thoughts continued to run through my mind. Would Cheyanne even know who I was? Would any of my friends come?

Maggie and Lisa tried to calm us down and assured us that everything would be okay. They remembered how they felt on their first Visiting Day four months ago. They had been worried about how their parents would treat them.

Maggie left home under pretty bad circumstances and hadn't been getting along with her parents. When they had seen the progress she made in such a short amount of time, they were so impressed. She still had a lot of work to do but showed them the respect they deserved. They could see hope in her eyes.

Lisa had gained such confidence in herself that her mother hardly recognized her. She greeted them with a smile and embraced them with open arms of gratitude for this opportunity for growth.

Hearing their experiences relieved some of the stress we were all feeling.

At ten o'clock that morning, the dinner bell rang, meaning it was time to join everyone at the main entrance of Everly Hall.

Just one short month ago we had all met here as strangers. Now we all stood united as we faced the unknown once again. Not only were we worried for ourselves, but we were concerned for those we now considered sisters. One last glance into each other's eyes, and the chaos began.

I was the first to see my family. Without warning, tears flowed from my eyes, and I ran into my daddy's outstretched arms.

His 6-foot 4-inch stature made it easy for me to spot him in the crowd. Standing next to him was my much shorter mother holding my baby sister in her arms.

Baby Cheyanne reached out her chubby little hands and babbled something that sounded a bit like "Aramie".

I swept her up into my arms and cried like I was the baby. From behind me came the familiar, "Hey, sis," from my older brother, Cody.

I turned to look at him as tears ran down both of our faces. He quickly wiped them away to avoid anyone seeing his emotions.

I glanced around to see if any of my friends had come. I was a little disappointed but knew better than to expect it. They had better things to do, and volleyball practice had started. Carrie Stevens had taken my place as captain and couldn't miss tryouts this weekend.

They stared in awkward silence for a minute shuffling back and forth.

"Hey, let's go have a look around," I said.

My mother gently held my hand. She wasn't letting go until she had to.

Her tender touch gave me comfort in knowing that I was indeed still loved and a part of this family. I had let them all down, but I still had their love and support.

I heard a shriek and saw Eevie running towards a little girl with pigtails.

"Sarah! What a surprise." Eevie swooped Sarah into her arms as she repeated, "Eebie! Eebie!"

Off to Sarah's side stood two women, her foster mother Sharon and Mrs. Redmond, waiting anxiously to greet her.

Once Eevie caught Mrs. Redmond's eye, she put Sarah down and fell into Mrs. Redmond's loving arms. The tears couldn't be held back any longer.

Sharon couldn't stand it anymore and wrapped her arms around both of them.

Eevie hadn't expected anyone to show up today. Seeing these familiar faces gave her the strength she needed to carry on in this journey. While Eevie was concerned about her mother, for now this reunion was all that mattered.

Afton stood alone feeling very insecure. For a second, she wondered if she'd be worth the drive. She tried to eat her bacon and eggs this morning but mostly just pushed them from side to side on the plate.

Afton gained almost five pounds in the month she had been here but remained far from her goal weight.

Being anxious about Visiting Day caused Afton to start purging again. We all tried to calm her down, but it was too easy for Afton to return to old habits. Her tank top and shorts were still too big for her, and she wondered what her mother would say.

Just then she heard someone yell her name from across the gravel parking lot. She turned to see Cerena and Lilly running towards her. Her parents and brother, Brody, were not far behind.

"They do care," she whispered to herself. "You look beautiful... and healthy," her mother said as she scanned her up and down. Mrs. Campbell quickly wrapped her arms around Afton and held her tightly. The anxiety melted away as they embraced.

"Let me have my turn," Cerena and Lilly shouted at the same time.

To have the support of not only her family but also her friends meant the world to Afton.

Jordan drove up for the celebration, and, as he left his car, he saw Kyla standing beside a tree with her arms resting on her now protruding belly.

Their eyes met.

Kyla was confused.

"Why are you here?" Kyla asked, without thinking.

"Well, I could turn around and leave if you want me to," Jordan replied.

Jordan was the last person Kyla expected to see today. But looking around, his was the only face she recognized.

"Don't be silly," she said. "I was just surprised to see you, that's all. I wasn't sure anyone knew where I went."

Jordan moved closer and spoke quietly in her ear.

"I would find you anywhere," he said as he moved toward Kyla and gave her a soft kiss on her cheek.

Kyla blushed as his hair brushed against her face.

"When you didn't show up at the back-to-school party, I went to Preston and asked him if he knew where you were," Jordan said. "He got all cocky and told me, 'Well, if I did my job on prom night, she's probably off somewhere hiding.' I put it all together and went to see your parents. They figured since we had been friends for so long, they could trust me."

Kyla turned her back and cried.

"I am so ashamed, Jordan," Kyla said through tears. "I thought he loved me, and all he did was use me to get popular as the new guy in town. I should have known better than to fall for him and his games. Now, look where it got me."

Jordan reached around her and wiped the tears from her cheek.

"Don't cry, I'm here," he said. "I'm not going anywhere this time."

Kyla buried her face in Jordan's shoulder and let the tears fall.

At one o'clock, the families gathered in the back courtyard to enjoy a barbeque lunch. I helped prepare the meal the day before as part of my community service.

All we had to do today was bring out the food and set it on the tables. Potato salad, chips and baked beans were placed on a serving table along with the paper plates, cups and plasticware.

Two dispensers were at the end of the table where one was filled with water, while the other contained lemonade. Hamburger and hotdog buns as well as condiments were on another table beside the grill.

Maggie and Lisa's fathers oversaw cooking burgers and hot dogs on the grill and happily yelled out instructions to the other dads standing by waiting to help.

Each family took their turn in line and found a place to sit at the picnic tables or on blankets scattered around the grass.

I motioned to Afton, Eevie and Kyla to join me and my family in a shady area under some trees. The morning had been so busy we hadn't had a chance to get acquainted with each other's families. I was anxious to meet their family members and friends who came to show their support and introduce them to mine.

Introductions were made as everyone gathered around. I noticed that there was just one young man with Kyla, and they were holding hands. I suspected that it was Preston but didn't think he'd have the nerve to show up here.

"Laramie, this is Jordan," Kyla said as they walked towards me.

"Nnnnice to meet you, Jordan," I stammered.

I looked at Kyla with a question in my eyes, and she just smiled back at me.

"So, what's the story with you and your siblings' names?" Kyla asked, changing the subject.

She was of course, referring to me, my brother, Cody, and my sister, Cheyanne.

"I'll let my mom tell the story," I said. "Hey, mom! Kyla wants you to tell your favorite story."

Dad rolled his eyes at me. My mom jumped up with excitement.

"Well," she excitedly began, "Funny you should ask."

By now Mom had the attention of everyone sitting at the picnic table. Cheyanne began to fuss, so I took the opportunity to hold her and calm her down.

Mom continued.

"So, when Laramie's father and I were dating, we lived in Wyoming," my mom said. "We were your typical high school sweethearts and did everything together."

Mom told of how following graduation, the couple chose to do some traveling.

"We talked about our future together and about raising a family," she said. "While we were stargazing one night, he held me close and asked me to marry him. I, of course, said 'yes'. We decided that no matter where we lived, we would give our children names of cities in Wyoming. That way we would always be reminded of our time together there."

Many "oohs" and "aahs" were heard from around the table as everyone applauded the love story. Dad reached over and gave Mom a big hug and a kiss.

Lunch finished up, and once again everyone went their separate ways for the afternoon to spend time catching up.

When the sun set, we gathered around the campfire for s'mores and roasting marshmallows. Someone started singing "Kumbaya", and we all joined in.

Ms. King spoke a few parting words, and tears were shed as we anticipated saying our goodbyes.

Parting words were shared with each other's guests in hopes of seeing them again next month.

It wasn't any easier letting our loved ones go a second time.

As I handed Cheyanne over to my mom, her little arms held-me tight.

"I wuv you," she said.

My eyes burned as I tried to hold back the tears. We embraced as a family, and they climbed into the now, not-so-new, car. I waved as they drove away down the dark, desert highway.

Chapter 11: My Journey: Laramie

My parents grew up in Sheridan, Wyoming. They were high school sweethearts and graduated in 1957. They married in 1958, while my father attended the University of Wyoming.

He pursued a degree in Business Management while my mother worked at a local laundromat to help cover living expenses.

During my father's freshman year, my mother became pregnant unexpectedly. My dad quit school to focus on working full-time at a car dealership. He always said how hard this was for him. He had planned on having his own business someday and a college education would have been beneficial.

My mom had a difficult pregnancy and was put on bed rest for the last two months to prevent premature labor. My brother, Cody, was born four weeks early at 4 lbs. 2 oz. As a result, his lungs didn't fully develop, and his doctors kept him in the hospital's neonatal intensive care unit for several weeks.

This unit was new to the hospital, and the staff was ill-prepared to care for premature babies.

However, Cody's nurse, Lydia, paid special attention to him and attended to his every need. During this time, my mother returned home where my grandmother took care of her. Father worked extra hours at the car dealership to cover the medical expenses.

When Cody was well enough to go home, grandma stayed to help so dad didn't have to worry about things at home. Eventually, my grandma left, and mom managed to take care of herself and Cody.

Mom became pregnant with me fairly soon after Cody was born. Again, it was a complicated pregnancy requiring bed rest. Dad looked for hospitals equipped to care for premature infants since it was likely that I would also be born early.

The Pennsylvania Hospital had the most advanced Neonatal Intensive Care Unit in the country. Though it would be risky for my mother to travel, the doctors decided it was the best option for her and her unborn baby.

With my mother six months pregnant, they moved across the United States from Laramie, Wyoming to Philadelphia, Pennsylvania. My mom flew in a medical airplane, and my dad, Cody, and my grandparents traveled in a rented U-Haul.

Once in Philadelphia, Dad got a job at a car dealership. Mom was placed in the hospital to be monitored, and my grandparents took care of Cody.

I was born at 30 weeks gestation, which is ten weeks too early. I weighed 3 lbs. 4 oz., but I was born in a hospital ready to care for me properly.

Incubators were plentiful by now. The doctors and nurses were all trained to help premature infants survive. I stayed in the NICU for the first 10 weeks of my life after which I was strong enough to go home.

My grandparents eventually returned to Wyoming, so my parents were left on their own to take care of two babies under the age of two.

Dad proved to be a natural salesman and did very well selling cars. After a few years he was promoted to manager allowing Mom to stay home and care for us.

There was always enough money for our needs but not always for our wants.

It was important that Cody and I maintained good grades in hopes of earning college scholarships.

As we got older, we were encouraged to try different sports. Cody tried baseball and basketball. He had never really caught up to the other boys his age, so football was not an option for him.

I tried softball and volleyball. At a young age, it was obvious that I was a natural at volleyball. I wasn't the tallest on the team, but I had spunk and could set that ball better than anybody.

By the time I was a freshman in high school, I was on the Varsity Team and already had scouts looking at me. I had kept a 4.0 GPA and was on track to receive both academic and volleyball scholarships from multiple colleges and universities.

During that same year, my mother got pregnant. She had been advised not to have more children due to her previous complications.

This time Mom's doctor immediately ordered her to bed rest.

I took care of her and often fixed dinner and did the laundry in addition to my homework and volleyball schedule.

Any kind of social life - other than volleyball - was out of the question. Because of this, I was seldom invited to parties or other high school activities.

I often felt depressed and alone. I knew it was important for me to ensure the health of my mother and future sibling, but I secretly wished for a "normal" life and best friends to share it with.

Finally, baby Cheyanne was born at 38 weeks. This was a miracle and a new record for my mother. Cheyanne was born healthy and did not require any time in the NICU. Yet, my parents were extremely overprotective of her, and no friends were allowed in our home.

There were times when I felt resentment towards Cheyanne.

It seemed as if my parents had no time for me anymore. To make things worse, money was tight.

Unless Dad sold a car, we lived paycheck to paycheck. As store manager he received a monthly salary that covered living expenses but not much else.

Gradually, I was able to participate in other activities besides my volleyball practices and games. I was even allowed to attend parties and hang out with my friends.

The day I was invited to go to the mall, I was beyond excited. I was finally one of the girls!

I felt a sense of freedom, but I also knew better than to ask for money to spend. It had been a long time since I had new clothes.

I was anxious to do some window shopping and maybe just try things on for fun.

Dad drove up the driveway that night in a new car he had earned by being top salesman of the year. It was supposed to be a celebration, but instead the day ended in tragedy.

That day is what brought me here to Everly Hall. I don't know what I was thinking. I had never even thought about stealing something.

The peer pressure got to me. I didn't have the courage to stand up for myself and for what I knew was right. The thought crossed my mind that maybe if I did something big then my parents would pay attention to me.

I will forever be sorry for what happened that day. Now I was paying for it.

Yet, meeting these wonderful girls at Everly Hall was the one positive outcome of it all.

My community service was intended to last six months. I didn't want to be away from home and volleyball any longer than necessary.

The more time away, the less my chances of a scholarship became. Luckily, there was a volleyball net set up outside. But winter was coming, and there wasn't much time left for outdoor activities.

My routine for the summer had been to keep up the outside recreation area and the inside game room.

As cooler days became more frequent, I focused more on the inside.

Puzzles and board games seemed to always need sorting on the shelves while arts and craft supplies needed to be restocked.

When there were special events, such as visiting days, I also helped in the preparation. It seemed a small price to pay for my mistakes.

One afternoon, all of that changed.

Reality set in.

Ms. King came to my room and announced that I would be going to the Freiburg State Fair the next day.

"That sounds fun!" I exclaimed. "Not for fun, Laramie. You will be there as a custodian."

I stood in silence.

"What exactly does that mean?" I asked.

She looked me squarely in the eye and explained my duties for the next three days. Those would include cleaning the restrooms, picking up garbage and making sure the livestock had water in their troughs.

I didn't know what to say.

"Pack your bags, you leave right after breakfast in the morning," Ms. King ordered.

She left the room and closed the door behind her.

The loud engine of the orange school bus pulling into the gravel driveway caused everyone to pause and stare out the window.

"What is that doing here?" asked Maggie.

Just then, Ms. King rose from her seat.

After clearing her throat, as she always did, she made an announcement.

"All community service girls may now leave and board the bus for the Freiburg State Fair," Ms. King said. "They will return in three days. Please say your goodbyes."

The ten of us took our dirty dishes to the kitchen and collected our bags. With heads buried in our sweatshirts, we climbed the steps onto the dirty smelly bus.

Feeling ashamed of what brought us to this point, we each found a seat and began the one-hour ride to our doom.

No words were exchanged, just looks of uneasiness and dread of the days to come.

We arrived at the fairgrounds and were directed to the trailer where we would be sleeping for the next two nights.

The trailer was an older model with bunk beds, a full-sized bed, and a dinette that folded out to create a bed.

To our delight, the trailer had a bathroom with a shower and running hot and cold water. At least we could be comfortable at night even if our days were especially unpleasant.

Just when we thought we could take advantage of some down time, we were greeted by our supervisor, Mr. Kent.

He directed us towards the public restrooms and pointed out the trash receptacles along the way. Across the fields were the livestock areas.

Five of the girls would oversee cleaning the stalls and making sure the animals had hay. The other five of us would need to fill the water troughs morning and night. All of us would keep the entire fairgrounds clear of trash. Thousands of people would flood the grounds over the coming days, and the job felt daunting.

While Mr. Kent noticed the looks we gave each other and the growing concern on each of our faces, he was undeterred.

"Good luck, ladies!" He turned and waved as he added, "People start arriving in 30 minutes."

We were exhausted by the end of our three-day sentence. Even the stinky school bus was a reprieve from what we had seen.

Our thin mattresses on the murphy beds felt like heaven. We slept like babies on our first night back.

Our normal routine quickly started all over again on Monday morning.

Sorting paint colors had never been so much fun!

Chapter 12: Afton's Journey

On the corner of State Street and Harrison Avenue in Boston is a ranch style house surrounded by a white picket fence and lush gardens.

The beautiful red brick home is a stark contrast to the traditional split-level houses surrounding it.

Charles Campbell purchased the property a few months back and had his family's home custom built by the best construction company in the Boston area.

Being the best and looking the best was important to the Campbells. Charles was Senior Partner at the law firm, Campbell, Tierney, and Waters. His wife, Vivian, served as president of the Ladies Society of Boston. They belonged to the local country club and participated in all local civic events.

Afton was a tall, blonde beauty with striking blue eyes. At 16-years-old, she stood at 5 feet and 10 inches. Her younger brother, Donny, 12, was a curly haired boy on the brink of growing into a handsome teenager. Both were popular at school and were always involved in sporting and social activities.

Although she was attractive and well liked, Afton never felt like she was enough.

Whenever she looked in the mirror, all she saw was an overweight, plain girl staring back at her.

One day, while feeling especially lonely and depressed, Afton ate an entire bag of chips and a full container of dip. Instead of feeling better, Afton felt guilty for devouring all that junk food and felt very sick and bloated.

Afton went into the bathroom. She knelt in front of the toilet as if praying for some type of answer and threw up everything she had just eaten.

It hurt.

Quickly, she turned on the faucet to drown out any sounds that could be heard coming from the bathroom.

Afton felt the strain in her face and stomach. She fell to the ground in complete exhaustion.

After a few painful minutes, she gained her composure, and Afton felt a little better.

Standing up to wash her face, she looked at the sorry looking stranger in the mirror staring back at her.

"What have I done?" she whispered.

Charles and Vivian Campbell were both raised in wealthy families. Their parents had been acquaintances and decided at an early age that the two of them would marry someday. They attended the same private school and went to all the same parties.

As they grew up, they recognized what was happening. Since their families had been together at almost every opportunity, it became apparent what their intention was.

The two of them developed a friendship over the years, and it felt natural to begin dating. The relationship turned into romance, and a few short years later, they were married.

The wedding had been the social event of the year.

The couple held their ceremony at the Cathedral of the Holy Cross, the largest Roman Catholic Church in New England.

The Boston Globe's Society section featured the wedding and showcased the photos of the prestigious guests in attendance.

 The young couple was thrown into the spotlight and expected to continue the elaborate lifestyles of their parents.

Charles Campbell attended Harvard Law School in Cambridge, Massachusetts. He was top in his class and graduated with honors. Vivian stayed home and participated in the luncheons and parties put on by her mother and mother-in-law. It was necessary to keep up appearances early to ensure they would be included in later years.

The newlyweds' parents gave them an upscale apartment to live in until Charles secured a job as an intern at a law firm. It wasn't long before he was hired as a junior attorney at Tierney and Waters. Within a few years he made partner.

He and Vivian decided to start a family, and soon welcomed a daughter, Afton. A son, Donny, was added to the family a few years later.

They were content with two children and were able to give them whatever they wanted.

Money and material things were easy to come by; yet, feeling loved unconditionally wasn't always the case.

Afton's best friend, Lilly, was constantly trying to lift her spirits. She invited her to parties and always reminded her of how attractive she was.

"All the girls are jealous of you and your beautiful, blonde hair and hourglass figure," Lilly often said.

These comments only made Afton feel more self-conscious and left her with the desire to lose more weight.

"If they want to be jealous, I'll give them something to be jealous about!" was her reply.

Afton attended parties and ate very little to keep up appearances. She would then go home and binge in her bedroom until she felt sick. Then she proceeded to vomit until there was nothing left.

This went on for nearly 18 months before anyone noticed. As long as she wore the same baggy clothes, her weight loss was kept hidden. Her mother suggested Afton buy some new clothes to show off her figure, but

Afton insisted her old clothes were fine. Vivian didn't like that response and insisted they go shopping.

While shopping, Vivian reached into the store's dressing room to hand Afton a blouse. There Vivian saw Afton's skeleton-like image in the mirror.

Vivian gasped, but quickly covered her mouth, so Afton wouldn't hear her. Vivian thought that maybe if she ignored it, it wouldn't be real.

"Surely, it couldn't be true. Why would Afton do such a thing? She has everything a girl could want," Vivian fretted.

The thoughts ran through Vivian's head as she waited for Afton to finish trying on the new clothes.

Afton emerged shyly from the dressing room to show her mother.

"Why, you look simply stunning!" her mother replied. "Let's go purchase these and then grab some lunch!"

The thought of food made Afton gag. Yet, she quickly agreed and changed into her old clothes while her mother paid for the new outfits.

Vivian chose to have lunch at a tea house located in the downtown district of Boston.

It was a sunny Saturday afternoon, so they ate outside on the terrace. From here, they could see the busyness of a spring day and watch people going about their weekend activities.

Vivian was quick to judge the clothes and hair styles of others as they walked by. Afton quietly observed as she slowly ate her Caesar salad and French onion soup.

"There is a new family that just joined the country club. Your father and I have arranged to have dinner with them next Friday night," Vivian said. "They have a daughter your age, Cerena, I think. It would be good for you to meet her and make her feel welcome."

As Vivian spoke, Afton remembered the new girl she met at a party the night before. She was the epitome of the upper class and quite frankly not Afton's type.

"Of course, mother," she grudgingly replied.

With lunch finished, mother and daughter located their Mercedes in the parking garage and drove home in silence.

The following days went by like any other week at school.

Cerena made herself known as the "new girl in town" and played the part well. She flirted with all of the basketball jocks and tried out for cheerleader for the upcoming school year.

Afton tried being cordial but found it difficult to even carry on a conversation with Cerena. It seemed that she only wanted to talk about herself. Afton was not looking forward to the dinner with their two families at the country club on Friday night.

Friday night came quicker than Afton would have liked. She, Vivian, Charles, and Donny, pulled up to the country club valet parking.

"Take good care of her," Charles said as he handed the keys to the driver.

The family climbed out of the car and proudly walked inside.

"Reservations for Campbell, please." Charles said.

The hostess quickly directed them to their table where the Carlton's were already seated. Mr. Carlton stood to shake Charles' hand.

"Nice to see you, Charles," Mr. Carlton said. "Thank you for the invitation. This is my wife, Nancy, and our daughter, Cerena."

The two ladies nodded, and the Campbells took the remaining seats. Afton and Cerena hardly spoke a word to each other while their parents carried on meaningless adult conversations.

As dinner was winding down, Afton excused herself and went to the restroom. After several minutes, Cerena decided to go check on her.

What Cerena discovered after entering the restroom would change the course of their friendship forever.

Chapter 14: Eevie's Journey

"It's a girl!" the doctor proclaimed, as he placed the screeching newborn on her mother's chest.

The dark, curly-haired baby gazed into her mother's frightened eyes looking for love and security.

Tears ran down Colleen Wright's face as she stared back at this tiny stranger she had just brought into the world.

At just 16 years old and still a child herself, the idea of raising a baby on her own terrified Colleen. Yet, the longer she held her, the calmer Colleen became.

"We can do this, little one," she promised her baby as Colleen gave her baby a kiss.

Colleen snuggled the infant in the hospital receiving blanket and softly began singing.

"Birdy, birdy, where's your nest? Birdy, birdy, where's your nest?" she sang.

The familiar lullaby her father had sung to her as a child brought her peace. The new mother and her baby girl fell into a deep sleep. The nurse gently took the baby from Colleen to check the newborn's vitals.

Colleen's doctor noted that she had such a quick delivery, it would require several stitches to repair the damage done to her body.

"You will need a few more days of rest in the hospital to recover," her doctor said.

Colleen sighed in relief as she needed all the help she could get. There was no one waiting at home to help her.

"Thank you, doctor," she said. "I so appreciate it."

The father of Colleen's baby knew nothing about the pregnancy.

"Let's just keep it that way," she said to herself.

After three days in the hospital, it was time for mama and baby to go home. The hospital staff had become very fond of the two of them, and it was hard to say goodbye.

The nurse brought in the birth certificate for Colleen to sign and verify the baby's name. While singing the lullaby to her baby that morning, Colleen decided to look up what name might mean "bird."

She came across the name, Evelyn, which means "strength, desired, or little bird."

The new mom instantly knew her baby would be called Evelyn Colleen. Her baby would give Colleen the strength she needed, and together they would learn to fly.

Colleen had been raised by her father after her mother became ill and passed away when Colleen was just seven years old.

Her daddy worked hard to provide for them, but it was hard being a single Black man raising a daughter on his own. He made sure she was clean and bought her nice clothes from a second-hand store.

Colleen's dad made friends with the owners who looked out for clothing in her sizes. Colleen's dad discreetly picked them up in the back alley after the store closed. Colleen never knew they were used and was happy to have a new dress to wear occasionally.

Then one day at school, a girl passed her in the hall and asked her where she got her dress.

"My daddy bought it for me. Isn't it lovely?" Colleen replied.

The girl grabbed her by the arm and ripped the sleeve.

"Oh, is that right?" she asked. "It was in my closet until a few days ago when my mother decided it wasn't good enough for me and too old and too worn to wear anymore!"

With a wicked laugh, the girl turned and walked away with her cruel classmates, leaving a sobbing Colleen alone in the hall.

Colleen never returned to school.

Instead, she taught herself from library books where she learned to read and to do math.

Colleen had learned enough at school in the first three grades to continue on her own. The librarian became her friend and often stayed after her shift to read to Colleen.

Being a child of color in the 60's wasn't easy. People were still adjusting to having blacks and whites congregate in public places.

Often, other library patrons stared at Colleen whenever she walked into the library. The friendly librarian would quickly direct her to a quiet place to read and study.

With Colleen's father working extra shifts, she was often left alone to fend for herself. The library became Colleen's safe place. Yet, as she grew older, Colleen became less interested in books, and, instead, went exploring after the library closed.

The streets of Boston were dark and scary at night, with shadows lurking around every bend. Strange voices, eerie sounds and blaring sirens filled the smokey alleys. Drug dealers and ladies of the evening occupied every corner waiting for eager customers.

Lonely and desperate, Colleen gave into her pursuers and decided to try just one of whatever it was they were selling that night.

She was euphoric.

It seemed as if all her cares gently melted away. Nothing seemed to matter. Just one taste slowly turned into a nightly habit, and soon she found herself craving it more and more.

When Colleen returned home late one night, her father asked her where she had been.

Colleen wobbled about. Her eyes were glazed over.

"You're high," he said.

"No, I'm not," she claimed.

"Then explain the red eyes and slurred speech," he demanded.

Colleen stumbled to her bedroom and collapsed onto the bed.

"If you're going to live this way, then you are no longer welcome here. Pack your bags and be gone first thing in the morning," her father said as he stormed out of her room, slamming Colleen's bedroom door shut.

When Colleen awoke the next morning, she knew she could either continue doing drugs or get clean. Both choices would have significant outcomes for the rest of her life.

She knew the easier choice would lead her down a long and winding road full of many troubles and lots of confusion. The harder choice would take courage and determination, Colleen thought.

Colleen pondered her decision, knowing which one was right. She also realized that it would be the more difficult path and wasn't sure she had the strength.

Climbing out of bed, Colleen was ready to face her father and let him know her plans.

Mr. Wright was reading the morning paper and drinking his morning cup of coffee. He raised his eyes and looked at Colleen as she entered the room.

"Well," he said. "What have you decided to do?"

"I want to get clean," was her reply.

With tear-filled eyes, Colleen explained how she needed his help to accomplish this difficult goal.

He stood up and put his arms around her.

"I'll be right by your side," he said softly.

Getting clean was even harder than she anticipated. Every day Colleen was approached by drug dealers pushing her to make a purchase.

Colleen's determination wavered, and she soon found herself in a rundown motel room. Frightened and alone, Colleen stayed in bed for several days. She felt terrible knowing she had just let go of all she had accomplished over the last few weeks. Colleen stayed inside the hotel room for a week leaving only for meals.

Colleen often thought about calling her father and telling him what happened, but she knew it would all lead to another fight. She was doing just fine out here, she told herself.

"I can do this. I will do this," she said.

Colleen's changed mindset helped her get a new, steady job. That money from her job also helped her purchase a membership at the local tennis club.

She was thriving until one rainy Thursday, four weeks into being drug-free.

Colleen had just got home from work with her paycheck in hand. She put the money in her special "Save Box" to take to the bank tomorrow and began getting ready for a late-night tennis match.

Just as Colleen grabbed her bag, she heard the shrill telephone ringing on the nightstand. She dropped her bag on the bed, and, thinking it was her tennis partner, Kate, answered it without hesitation.

"Hello?" she said. "I'm looking for Colleen Wright. Are you associated with Joseph Wright?"

"Yes, I am Colleen Wright, his daughter," she said. "How may I help you?"

"Miss Wright, I'm Robert Tierney, an attorney from Tierney and Waters Law firm," he said. "Your father, Joseph Wright, was involved in an accident involving a drunk driver this evening. He arrived at the St. Alphonsus hospital but was too injured to save. I am sorry for your loss, Colleen."

Colleen dropped the phone and collapsed onto the floor. Tierney continued talking, explaining that the drunk driver who hit her dad had also died.

"Miss Wright, Miss Wright, are you still there?" he continued.

Tierney persisted in calling out her name, but eventually hung up.

Colleen remained on the floor for several minutes trying to process what she had just heard. The silence quickly turned into loud, eerie screaming.

"No! No! It can't be true," she shrieked. "Daddy, you can't leave me now. I've come so far, and I need you."

Time screeched to a standstill, and everything felt surreal.

After what felt like hours, Colleen picked herself up off the floor and reached for the phone. She needed to hear the news again to verify what she thought he said. In hopes that it had been a nightmare, Colleen walked to the motel's office to ask if they had a way of tracing incoming calls.

"It shows that the call came from Tierney and Waters Law. Would you like for me to dial it for you?" asked the hotel clerk.

"If you don't mind, yes, please," Colleen replied quietly.

A cheerful voice answered the phone, irritating Colleen.

She cleared her throat.

"My name is Colleen Wright. I received a call earlier regarding my father, Mr. Joseph Wright," she whispered.

The woman on the line asked her to please repeat herself. Gathering strength, Colleen told her why she was calling.

"Please hold the line while I get someone to talk to you," she said.

Robert Tierney answered and confirmed what he had told her earlier. He instructed her to come to his office and complete the necessary paperwork.

After getting the address, Colleen called a taxi.

Before going to the attorney's office, Colleen went to the morgue to identify her father. Staring at his battered body, childhood memories flashed before her eyes. He had been a good father and gave her a decent life while being a single parent.

It hadn't always been easy, especially after she started doing drugs. It could have been different for them, but her life's choices ruined any chance of having a "normal" life.

Colleen declared that this man was, indeed, her father and signed the death certificate. She returned to the taxi and gave the driver the address of the law office.

Joseph Wright had very little to leave for his daughter.

They lived frugally and had just enough to get by. He was renting an apartment so there was no home left for her to inherit or to live in. Whatever was left in the apartment when he left that evening was all she had to remember him by.

Colleen gathered his few belongings and returned to her motel room. No sooner had she unlocked the door, when she vomited.

The day's events were too much for her. Recalling what happened that day made Colleen sick to her stomach.

Or so she thought.

Then Colleen remembered that she was a few days late on her cycle.

"How could that be?" she mumbled to herself.

She recalled waking up alone in the motel room but didn't know how she got there. Flashes of a White man's face appeared in her memory. But who was he? Why was he there with her? Thoughts of the unthinkable crossed her mind.

Colleen ran to the front desk to ask if anyone knew who had taken her there. No one could recall that particular night.

She asked them to check the register, but all they saw was a "John Doe."

Sobbing, she hailed a taxi and went to the nearest emergency room.

Once there, she told the workers she hadn't had a period in months and was admitted for a pregnancy test and exam.

The results were positive.

Colleen was six weeks pregnant.

What was she going to do?

Colleen had no family to help and didn't even know who the father was. Abortion wasn't legal, and besides that, she would never even consider it.

There was no other choice than to keep the baby, Colleen said.

The following years were excruciatingly hard as Colleen found herself on a roller coaster of drugs making it impossible for her to care for Eevie.

The state eventually got involved and placed Eevie into protective foster homes.

Being tossed from house-to-house left Eevie feeling empty with no sense of what a family really was.

At one point, Colleen got clean, and Eevie returned home to live with her. It seemed as if life might turn around for them, but then Colleen learned she could make a lot of money by making and selling drugs.

By the time Eevie was 15 years old, they were running a full-fledged meth lab in their house.

The day of the fire was the last straw. The two of them may have had their last chance at a lifetime together.

Chapter 15: Kyla's Journey

"**K**yla Jane, where are your shoes?" Kyla's mother yelled frantically.

"We're going to be late for your first day of kindergarten!"

The first day of school made Kyla very nervous.

She had not attended preschool and was not used to being with large groups of children, or large groups of any kind really. Being an only child, she was often left alone to pretend and play with her imaginary friends.

Mr. and Mrs. Armstrong were constantly caught up in their own private world.

Not that Kyla was ignored or neglected, she had every material thing a little girl could ask for. In fact, she had a whole room filled with toys, books, stuffed animals and art supplies. The problem was that she had no one to share it with.

When Kyla was just 5 years old, her father ran for mayor of the small town of Quincy, just outside Boston. Getting started in politics required a lot of social events and gatherings. This meant there were several nights a week when Kyla would have a babysitter.

Most of the babysitters just sat on the phone all night talking to their boyfriends. Occasionally, one would play house or Barbies with her, but usually it wouldn't last very long.

They were one of the few families with a television set, so teenage girls were more interested in watching new Star Trek or Mission Impossible episodes than in watching Kyla. As a result, Kyla promised herself that, when she grew up, she would be a great babysitter.

Thomas Armstrong had been involved in high school and college politics.

In high school, he had been both the Sophomore and Junior Class President. In his senior year the student body voted him as their president. Being involved in high school politics got him interested in serving on the executive board at a college level.

Thomas attended Northeastern University in Boston and majored in Political Science. He received his bachelor's degree in business administration and a Masters in Political Science. During his years at the university, he served as Student Senator on the University Student Executive Board. This opportunity gave him a look at how local government was run and piqued his interest to learn more.

Soon after graduating from college, Tom Armstrong started his own business operating a delivery truck service. Thanks to his business degree Tom had the knowledge he needed to own a company.

He became very well known as an honest businessman with integrity. His customers encouraged him to run for office. Tom decided he wanted to make a difference at the city level and chose the office of mayor. He could continue supervising his business while serving in local politics.

Mrs. Armstrong pulled the car out of the garage and honked one more time.

Kyla came running with one shoe on and one shoe still in her hand. She climbed into the back seat and squirmed about until her errant shoe was finally on her foot.

She reached over and closed the door. Folding her arms across her chest, she stuck her lip out and pouted all the way to the schoolhouse.

Her mother tried to engage in small talk about the excitement of the first day of school, but Kyla sat quietly.

Eventually, they arrived, and Mrs. Armstrong pulled into a parking space in front of the school.

Mrs. Armstrong walked around to let Kyla out, but Kyla refused to move.

"Get out of the car, Kyla. The bell is about to ring," Mrs. Armstrong urged. She was losing her patience and gave Kyla a stern look.

Slowly Kyla slid to the end of the seat and made her way out of the car. Grabbing hold of her mother's hand, they sauntered to the front door.

Children were frantically running down the halls hoping to beat the tardy bell. The kindergarten teacher, Miss Wells, stood at the doorway waiting to greet the timid and scared new students.

"Good morning," she said kindly, as she stretched out her hand to welcome Kyla.

Kyla looked up and stared into her gentle brown eyes. She placed her tiny hand in hers and walked into the classroom.

"I think we're going to be just fine," Miss Wells said as she motioned to Mrs. Armstrong to leave.

Kyla learned to read her own name long before she started kindergarten and quickly found a seat with her name on it.

Next to her sat a little boy. He looked as scared as she felt. His name tag said, "Jordan." He had brown hair and pale blue eyes peering from behind silver aviator glasses and was wearing a Lone Ranger T-shirt.

He sat quietly with his hands folded in front of him.

Kyla glanced around the room at the bright colors and the alphabet chart mounted on the wall. She quietly began singing her "A, B, C,'s" and noticed Jordan hesitatingly joining in.

Before long, all the children were happily singing along. Miss Wells clapped her hands in approval.

"Well done, students," she said.

Jordan smiled over at Kyla and never left her side for the rest of the day. He needed her as much as she needed him.

Jordan and Kyla played together every day, and they stayed friends through their elementary school years.

Thanks to kindergarten, Kyla was no longer the quiet, little girl with no friends to share her toys with.

Her playroom became the hub of play dates and birthday parties.

Mrs. Armstrong loved hosting afternoon garden parties with the children's mothers.

It proved to be a gateway into the high society social clubs she would eventually become a part of.

Tom became Mayor of Quincy and served for four years. Kyla attended some of the town meetings and became interested in politics herself.

Even at a young age, Kyla was intrigued by what was happening in her community. The rise in drug abuse and teen pregnancies caused her great concern. She wished there was something she could do.

When elections were announced for Jr. High officers, Kyla jumped at the opportunity. Maybe by being a good example to her peers, she could make a difference.

Jordan agreed to be her campaign manager, and he quickly rounded up other kids to be on her team.

Posters were made that read, "Kyla Arm 'strong' for 8th grade Class President. She's built for the job!"

There was a picture of an arm flexing its muscles indicating her strength and determination. She presented a compelling speech and drew in the majority of her classmates' votes over her rival, Yolinda Gates.

As was customary at the time, the runner-up became vice-president. Yolinda was discouraged about the outcome, but over time she learned to make the most of it.

Kyla included her in many of the major decisions and was sure to listen to her concerns and suggestions. The two of them made a great pair and decided to run for office again together when they entered high school.

During their freshman year they worked together as secretary and treasurer for the student body.

After surviving the trenches of junior high, Kyla and Jordan remained good friends. Jordan was always there when Kyla needed him. If a boy broke her heart, he was there to pick up the pieces.

By their freshman year, Jordan realized his feelings for her had changed. He didn't want to be the guy who healed her broken heart anymore. He wanted to be the one holding her in his arms late at night.

Kyla started seeing him differently too.

Jordan recently shed his glasses for contact lenses, and suddenly Kyla found him very attractive. Her heart beat faster when she was with him. Doing homework was no longer enough.

They yearned to be with each other.

Sitting at a desk across the classroom was almost unbearable. They passed notes to each other during Math and English classes and met at their lockers in between periods.

Other boys would ask Kyla out, but she never said "yes".

She preferred to be with Jordan, and he felt the same way. The days of being the shy, lonely girl she once was, were long gone. Jordan helped her come out of her shell, maybe even too much.

When she wasn't with Jordan, Kyla was involved in student government activities. She and Yolinda were always busy with school improvements or a city service project.

Kyla also spent hours babysitting.

She remembered being so lonely as a child when her parents were out for the night.

The financial benefits were great, but most of the time she sacrificed her 25 cents an hour and did it as a kind gesture to help a couple who needed some grown-up time out of the house.

The children loved her, and she couldn't help but think that she might make a good mother someday.

Near the end of freshman year, elections were held for sophomore class president. Kyla and Yolinda decided to run against each other this time. They were both aware of what the consequences could be as a result of this decision but were willing to take the chance.

As always, Jordan was Kyla's campaign manager and kept everything running smoothly.

Yolinda had learned the ropes by now and had a competitive team on her side. Posters were hung and a week of campaigning pursued to sway the votes in one direction or the other.

On Friday, an assembly was held where the candidates presented their speeches full of goals for the upcoming school year.

Yolinda went first and promised better lunches, more assemblies and less light at the dances. The last one earned a cheer from the student body but a groan from the staff. She concluded by saying she would be the best Sophomore class president there had ever been at Freeport High School.

When it was Kyla's turn, she stood up proudly and approached the stage. Her long skirt got caught on the steps and she clumsily fell to the floor. Everyone laughed, everyone except Jordan. He rose to his feet and swiftly ran towards her.

The gym went eerily silent as he helped her finish her way up the stairs. Kyla had mascara running down her cheeks, and there was dirt from the dusty gym floor on her new skirt. She stood shaking at the pulpit.

Jordan stayed close by to support her in case she lost her balance. She searched her mind for the words she had prepared but found nothing.

Each candidate was allowed three minutes for their speech. Kyla's time was running out.

Jordan stood in front of the microphone and faced the student body.

"You all know what kind of person Kyla is. She has served you well before, and she will again. Please vote for Kyla Armstong," Jordan said.

Jordan took her by the hand, and they exited from the stage. The room remained silent.

The votes were tallied over the weekend. Jordan tried to keep Kyla's mind off the election, but with Kyla's swollen knee bothering her, it wasn't an easy task.

They couldn't go for a walk because it hurt too bad. They couldn't go to a movie because Kyla's knee hurt too much to bend it. All they could do was listen to their favorite music.

So, Jordan went to the record store and bought the new Wings album, "Band on the Run." Lying on the couch snuggling turned into an afternoon well spent.

On Sunday he called to see how she was feeling. The swelling had gone down, and she thought she would be fine for school on Monday.

When her mother called her to the phone a second time, Kyla was pleasantly surprised to hear Yolinda's voice on the other end of the line.

"How are you feeling?" she asked in a subdued tone. "I am so sorry for what happened at the assembly on Friday. I hope you can make it to school tomorrow for the announcement of the class elections."

Kyla wasn't quite sure what to say.

"Thank you for calling. I'll be there, and may the best man ... or woman win," she said. "See you tomorrow then, have a good evening."

Yolinda hung up the phone on the other end of the line, and Kyla put the handle down on the phone rest. It was getting late, so she made her way down the hall to her bedroom.

After a restless night, her alarm startled her when it went off at seven a.m.

Forgetting that her knee was sore, she jumped from her bed only to fall to the floor. Gathering herself, she stood and limped to the bathroom.

"I have to go to school today," she said out loud to herself while looking in the mirror.

Barely able to stand long enough to shower, Kyla wrapped herself in a towel and proceeded to blow dry her hair.

She was grateful that her mother had bought her the latest in hair tools. It made it easier to get ready in a short amount of time.

Kyla found an ace bandage wrap under the bathroom sink and wrapped it around her knee for support. She then found a skirt just long enough to cover it.

A lightweight blouse finished off the ensemble. She walked into the kitchen with just enough time for hot pancakes before heading out the door to catch the bus.

The bus pulled forward into its place in line to unload the kids. The excitement of this morning's assembly made them more anxious than usual to start a Monday morning.

Everyone was eager to hear the results of the elections.

After checking into homeroom for roll call, the students filled the gym bleachers in anticipation of the announcements.

Julia Montgomery, the Student Body President, stood and led them in the Pledge of Allegiance.

When everyone had finally settled down, Mrs. Mowery came to the pulpit.

"As your Student Council Advisor, it is my privilege to announce next year's officers. We will start with the Freshman class," Mrs. Mowery said.

Time seemed to move very slowly as she read the names of the winners.

Cheers came from the students showing their approval, while others sat in silence over the disappointment of losing.

Kyla sat next to Jordan, holding his hand tightly. She almost forgot to breathe while waiting to hear the results for the Sophomore class.

"And your sophomore class president is…. Yolinda Gates!" Mrs. Mowery proclaimed in a booming voice.

Kyla looked at Jordan in disbelief and let go of his hand. Slowly she turned and walked out of the gym alone and discouraged.

Jordan stayed until the end of the assembly and then went straight to Kyla's locker.

He found her curled up on the floor sobbing.

"What did I do wrong?" she sniffed and looked up at him.

"You didn't do anything wrong. You'll always be a winner in my book," Jordan said as he sat down next to her and put his arm around her.

They sat on the floor wrapped in each other's arms until the bell rang, and they went to Math class hand in hand.

Kyla was nominated by the teachers to be a class ambassador. Though not as involved as usual, she still participated in school functions and assisted the staff with dances and other special events.

Her desire to be Junior Class President increased as she saw the need for better student leadership.

Yolinda did her best to keep her campaign promises, but most of it was really out of her hands.

School lunch would never get any better!

The school year was coming to an end, and Jordan and Kyla spent less and less time together.

Elections were held for next year's officers and as usual, Jordan was Kyla's campaign manager.

After last year's disaster, he did everything he could to make sure Kyla won.

She chose to wear a shorter skirt this year for the assembly, not only to ensure she didn't trip, but also because fashions had changed.

Yolinda's family would be moving over the summer, so Sandy Nichols was Kyla's opponent.

It was her first time participating in student elections, and Sandy wasn't prepared for all that it involved.

This along with Kyla's previous experience gave her the advantage. The two candidates gave their promissory speeches, and the students were dismissed to vote in their homeroom classes.

They would announce the winners at the end of the school day. At least Kyla didn't have to wait all weekend this year.

During 7th period, the principal's voice came blaring over the loudspeaker.

"Mrs. Mowery has some important news you have all been waiting for," he said.

"Good afternoon students, I have the results from today's election," she read through the younger classes and then said, "Now we have the results for the junior class."

She revealed the winners for secretary, treasurer, vice-president and finally...Jr. Class President.

"This year's winner is, Kyla Armstrong."

Kyla's classroom exploded with cheers of congratulations. Kyla searched the room for Jordan, but he left earlier to allow her to celebrate with her friends.

She felt alone even though she was surrounded by her classmates.

More and more time elapsed between their dates, and eventually Kyla and Jordan just stopped seeing each other. Neither of them could really say why, but the attraction seemed to fade.

When he reached for her hand, she quickly pulled it away. There was no passion in their good night kisses.

Kyla's mind was focused on planning for next year's school activities. Junior class president was a big responsibility. Kyla didn't want to let anyone down, and she couldn't be distracted by anyone.

One of the big fundraisers for prom was a car wash.
Kyla and her friends spent weeks putting up posters and
handing out flyers to local businesses.

Besides being a great way to earn money, it was going to
be a fun day in the summer sun before heading back to
school in a few short weeks.

When Kyla put on her new yellow bikini top and jean
shorts that morning, she had no idea how that day would
change the rest of her life.

Chapter 16: Gratitude and Thanksgiving

Hues of red, orange, and yellow covered the horizon as the leaves changed, and the chilly days of Fall settled in.

Laramie soaked in the beauty of Fall.

"It's my favorite time of year," she thought. "I can see why the Everlys chose this location."

Laramie smiled as she recalled the numerous times Ms. King told the girls about Mr. and Mrs. Everly getting married here and then finding the property for sale years later.

The autumn nights meant time spent around the campfire telling ghost stories and toasting marshmallows.

We started our school routine, so nights were cut short except on the weekends. We always looked forward to the first weekend of the month because we got to see family and friends.

My parents and siblings came every month to show their support. My six months had passed quickly. Although I didn't necessarily enjoy my community service hours, I learned to love the people I served each day.

I was anxious to be home with my family, but I was going to miss these girls so much. They showed me what true friendship looked like.

There was no judging or name calling. Someone always had your back and was there when you needed a shoulder to cry on.

Maggie and Lisa were going home.

The week before we started classes, they got the news. We all knew it was coming but weren't sure of their departure dates.

We spent every spare minute with them making lasting memories. Mrs. King even let us have a sleepover in the meeting area on their last night. Usually, we weren't allowed to sleep anywhere except in our own rooms, so it was quite a surprise and a delight!

We talked deep into the night and promised we would never forget each other. Our experiences at Everly Hall would forever change our lives.

Maggie and Lisa were leaving as different people than when they arrived. Maggie learned to control her temper and to express her feelings in a way that produced positive results.

"The light is back in your eyes!" her mother told her.

Lisa gained confidence in herself that she didn't know she was capable of. She walked with her shoulders back and her head held high. Her smile lit up any room she entered, and everyone wanted to be by her side.

While both girls were excited to be going home, they were also nervous and hesitant about returning.

"What would people say?" they both said time and time again.

It would take some time for people to accept them for who they had become and put their pasts behind them.

During their time at Everly Hall, Maggie and Lisa were surrounded by other teenage girls who were also struggling. Each day they encouraged one another to keep on striving for their best self.

"Who would be their cheerleaders once they got home?" they often asked Ms. King.

Ms. King assured them they were ready.

She rang the dinner bell to call us all together. With tears in her eyes, Ms. King called the girls by name and asked them to come to the front.

Holding hands, the two of them approached the small stage where Ms. King stood. She held two rolled up scrolls.

"I present to you Maggie Robbins and Lisa Simmons, our two most recent graduates of the Everly Hall School for Girls," she announced.

Mrs. King handed one scroll to Maggie and instructed her to open it and to read it aloud.

"This certificate of graduation is presented to Maggie Robbins," Maggie read. "In addition to passing all qualified courses with a 3.8 GPA, we also give her the 'Lamb' award for coming in as a lion and leaving like a lamb."

The audience laughed and gave her a round of applause. Holding back the tears, Maggie and Ms. King embraced.

Lisa followed Maggie's example, untied the scroll, and began reading.

"This certificate of graduation is presented to Lisa Simmons," she read. "In addition to her passing all qualified courses with a 3.6 GPA, we also give her the 'Lion' award for finding her voice and having the courage to share it with all of us."

Again, the audience roared with laughter as Ms. King wrapped her arms around Lisa.

Maggie and Lisa's families stood in the back of the room patiently waiting for them to say their farewells.

Afton, Eevie, Kyla, and I were the last to say good-bye. We held off as long as we could, but Ms. King motioned to us that it was time.

The six of us grabbed hands, just as we did on that first night together.

The last three months certainly proved what real friendship was. It was all about accepting people where they were and loving them anyway. Yet, it was also about helping them to achieve their goals and grow along the way.

Tears stung our eyes, and we knew we had to let go.

One by one, we released hands and watched as Maggie and Lisa joined their families and disappeared down the dusty driveway.

We watched until the dust settled, and they were out of sight. In a few short months, we would do it all over again.

Sunday was a day of rest as we adjusted to the new normal without Maggie and Lisa. The day was subdued and quiet.

We gathered in the lounge area and snuggled under cozy blankets where a blazing fire kept us warm. Soothing music played on the radio as we reminisced about our time together.

Monday morning and 6:30 came too early, and our new school routines began. Breakfast was served at 7 a.m. and classes began an hour later. We scattered to our various classrooms.

Some of us went to reading, writing and arithmetic while others went to life skills classes. After lunch, the rotation reversed.

Mary, from registration, was our education advisor. She made learning a fun and interactive experience. Most of us were sophomores or juniors in high school, so the curriculum was nearly the same. If alterations were necessary, accommodations were made.

I was a senior this year, so my work was a little more advanced. I wanted to be on track when I returned after Christmas break to graduate with my classmates in May.

I was beginning to realize that they weren't the best examples of what a friend should be, but I did grow up with them and wanted to share this milestone.

Kyla's baby bump continued to grow. She could feel the baby moving now and often hollered at us to come and put our hands on her pear-shaped belly.

Being in her second trimester, Kyla didn't get sick nearly as often and enjoyed participating in most activities. She was getting attached to the baby, but she knew she couldn't keep "him."

Kyla had been thinking about her options and discussed the possibility of adoption for her baby with Ms. King. She agreed to help Kyla find a family - if that was what she decided to do.

Afton reminded Kyla that her father was an attorney and could manage the legal aspects involved. Knowing what a kind man he was, made the idea easier for Kyla to consider.

The concept of open adoption was just starting to be discussed in the adoption world.

Open adoption would allow Kyla to participate in choosing the adoptive parents for her baby and also to remain a part of his life. The thought of never seeing her baby again frightened Kyla. Yet, she didn't care if she ever laid eyes on Preston again.

With the impending birth of her baby, Ms. King required Kyla to take Childbirth 101. There were ten girls in this class expecting babies in the next five months.

Miss Adeline, the nurse, and teacher gently explained the development of the growing baby and eventually the birthing process. Kyla and the other girls were a bit squeamish after watching the film on childbirth.

"I'm not sure I'm ready for this," Kyla said under her breath as she looked away.

Afton was learning good eating habits and gaining weight. It was difficult for her to watch the number climbing on the scales, but knew it was for her own good.

After seeing her progress on visiting day, Afton's mother left some money with Ms. King to purchase new clothes for Afton.

Afton was excited to go shopping. She invited Kyla to go with her. When Afton reached her goal of 110 pounds, Ms. King took the two of them into Boston for a shopping spree. Kyla was outgrowing her clothes too and needed to update her wardrobe.

With permission from Mary and Miss Adeline, Eevie and I got some of the girls to help us decorate for a Halloween party. While I was cleaning the attic as part of my service hours, I found a box of festive decorations and colorful costumes. I was anxious to share it.

By the time Ms. King and the two girls returned, the meeting room had been transformed into a haunted mansion. They walked into the dark room and reached for the switch to turn the light on.

A wet, wrinkled hand grabbed Afton's arm, and she let out a frightened scream.

"What was that?" she stammered.

Jumping back, she fell into Eevie's lap, and they both laughed hysterically. Giggles and snickering filled the meeting room as bodies tripped over each other frantically in the dark.

Suddenly, Ms. King whistled to get everyone's attention. The girls froze in their tracks and listened intently as she spoke.

"Nobody move! Before someone gets hurt, we need to find some light," Ms. King said.

I quickly ran to the fuse box and restored light into the room. When I returned, Ms. King was staring straight at me.

"This isn't what it looks like, Ms. King," I stammered.

"What exactly is it then, Laramie?" she asked, trying to hold back the laughter.

"We wanted to surprise you, that's all. It got a little out of hand, I guess," Laramie said.

Ms. King looked around the room at the worried faces.

"I say we all go to our rooms and get our costumes on. It's time for a real Halloween celebration!" Ms. King exclaimed.

The girls let out squeals of excitement as they scattered down the hall to their individual rooms. I picked up the box of costumes. Eevie and Afton helped me distribute them to the remaining girls in the meeting room.

We gathered in my room and proceeded to change into our costumes.

I found a pointy hat, a black dress and gloves and decided on being the traditional witch. Eevie gathered ears, paws, and a tail for a cat. Afton saw some wings and ballet shoes for the perfect fairy, and, of course, Kyla was an orange pumpkin.

After applying the appropriate make-up, we all returned to the eerie meeting room. Scary music played hauntingly in the background, and the door squeaked as we opened it.

"Boo!" a ghost popped out in front of us.

We all screamed and grabbed onto each other tightly. Another ghost appeared and then a third. Terrified, we continued walking toward the bright light that shone in front of the room.

"Greetings goblins," came a deep ghastly ghostly voice from behind the stage curtain. We recognized it as Ms. King, and our nerves settled.

"Please help yourselves to the treats and enjoy the music and games. The party will end at 11 o'clock sharp," she said.

We had more fun than we'd had in a long time. It was good to be silly and forget what brought us all here. Most of the other pregnant girls turned in at 10:00, but the rest of us partied until Miss Adeline escorted us out.

Ms. King let us sleep in the next morning. It was a much-needed rest. Yet, the mess from the night before stared us in the face when we arrived for breakfast. Our morning was spent cleaning the aftermath of our follies.

******

Thanksgiving brought our families for a special "Visiting Day." We prepared the traditional Thanksgiving feast and enjoyed spending time with our loved ones. We expressed gratitude to them for their continued support.

In addition to her family and Jordan, Kyla had an unwelcome guest.

It was Preston.

"Preston, what are you doing here?" a shocked Kyla demanded after seeing him.

"Well, since I had to find out about our baby from someone else, I thought I'd come see for myself." He smugly and sarcastically replied.

"I see by that fat belly of yours that I did my job! When is the kid coming anyway?" cocky Preston said.

Kyla slapped him while the other girls looked on in shock.

Ms. King heard the commotion and raced to Kyla's side.

"May I help you with something, young man? I haven't seen you here before," she said.

"I am the father of this girl's baby," Preston replied gruffly while scowling at Kyla. "I have every right to be here!"

Kyla's father stepped forward and interrupted.

"You are certainly not welcome here! Kindly, be on your way," Kyla's father said.

"Kyla, tell them all how much you love me and want us to be together." Preston said smugly as he smirked.

"Preston, I do not love you, and I never want to see you again!" Kyla responded through her tears and backed away from the boy.

Mr. Campbell, Afton's father, walked over.

"May I offer a suggestion?" he asked. "Why don't we go somewhere private and discuss this?"

"Mr. Campbell is an attorney, Preston," Ms. King said. "That might be a good idea."

Mr. Campbell pointed to a room away from the crowd and motioned to Preston and Kyla's family to join him.

They all slowly, cautiously followed.

Jordan held Kyla's hand and gave her a reassuring look that everything would be okay.

Kyla's parents huddled around Kyla protecting her from Preston.

"Preston, though this may be your child, Kyla has made it very clear that she wants nothing to do with you," Mr. Campbell said. "She has indicated to me that she would like to place the baby for adoption. In order to do that, you will need to relinquish your parental rights."

"You made this decision without me?' How dare you, you. . . you tramp!" Preston yelled as he threw up his hands in disgust.

Kyla gritted her teeth and slapped Preston again.

"You slut!" Preston said as he touched his now very bruised face.

"How dare you!" she cried. "You left me alone to deal with this, making no effort to contact me or see how I was doing. As I see it, it's better this way."

"You'll be hearing from my lawyer," Preston yelled as he turned and stomped away.

Moments later we heard his car speed away.

Kyla's parents comforted her by wrapping their arms around her. Jordan continued to hold her hand tightly. They returned to join the others in the dining hall for the Thanksgiving feast.

Eevie, Afton, and I ran to Kyla and hugged her.

"I can't believe he showed up here. The nerve!" Kyla said as she grabbed her stomach and cried in pain."

"Something is wrong!"

"Let's get her to a chair, please help me," Miss Adeline said as she quickly ran to Kyla.

Kyla's father gently helped her sit down in a nearby chair. She continued to breathe heavily.

The fear rose in Kyla as she shook like a leaf. We all stood in shock, unaware of what was happening and not knowing what to do.

Miss Adeline checked Kyla's pulse and noticed that it was quite fast.

"Laramie go get my medical bag," she asked me. "It's in my office right next door."

When I returned, Miss Adeline placed a blood pressure cuff around Kyla's arm.

"One hundred sixty over ninety-eight," she said. "That is quite elevated. We should probably call an ambulance."

Ms. King grabbed the phone and called an ambulance. Jordan helped Kyla to a couch in the reception area and tried to keep her comfortable.

Periodically Kyla cried out in pain. I reached for her hand and gave it a squeeze to reassure us both.

The ambulance arrived and whisked Kyla away. Miss Adeline rode along with her. The Armstrongs and Jordan drove in their car and met them at the hospital.

The rest of us stayed behind anxiously awaiting a phone call. We finished eating dinner and said goodbye to our families.

******

Eevie's foster mom, Sharon, brought Sarah to celebrate the holiday. She was growing up and learning to talk more clearly. Sharon shared her mother Colleen's progress and gave updates on the court proceedings.

Colleen had completed her classes but was waiting for a hearing date on the manslaughter charges. Eevie hoped to go see her in jail before long.

Sharon hugged Eevie and picked up Sarah to give her a kiss on the cheek.

"Goodbye, Eevie," she said quietly.

I was happy to see my parents, my brother and baby sister.

I realized how much I had to be thankful for.

My family stood up for me when no one else would. The people I thought were my friends had let me down. I was starting to worry about what my return to school would look like.

Afton was careful with how much she ate but made sure to eat enough for her necessary daily caloric intake. Her mother was so proud of her and continuously praised her. It made Afton a bit self-conscious, but she understood that it was her mother's way of acknowledging Afton's progress. Afton was wondering how she was going to handle life back at home.

After the "goodbyes" were said, it was time to clean up. Ms. King let us take a brief rest before digging into the piles of dirty dishes waiting for us.

Shortly after, we returned to our rooms, we received word that Kyla was on her way back from the hospital. Instead of resting, we anxiously awaited her arrival.

Kyla came directly to our room, and had her mother help her into the bed. While Kyla was pale and exhausted, she and her unborn baby would be fine.

The doctor placed her on bed rest for the following two weeks in hopes of lowering her blood pressure. He also started her on blood pressure medication that was safe for the unborn baby.

Knowing she was safe, we welcomed Kyla home and made our way to the kitchen to clean up.

With Kyla on bed rest, we would have added duties for a couple of weeks - maybe even longer if necessary. But we were all willing to pitch in to ensure the health of both Kyla and the baby.

That night, Eevie, Afton, and I, gathered around Kyla's bed and held hands in gratitude for life's blessings.

"Heavenly Father, we thank thee for the outpouring of blessings we received today," I prayed. "We are grateful for the love of families and friends. Most importantly, we are thankful for Kyla's safe return to us and for doctors who cared for her and her baby. In Jesus's name, Amen."

"I am very blessed, but this isn't 'my' baby," Kyla thought.

Exhausted from the events of the day, Eevie and Afton went to their room for the night. I had barely closed my eyes when I heard Kyla snoring.

"Good night," I said.

Chapter 17: The Holiday Season

We woke up to a snow-covered winter wonderland.

"There's something about the first snow of the season," mused Laramie "It always brings back memories of snow angels and ice skating in the park."

The Christmas holiday was approaching, and Everly Hall was decked out in festive decorations.

Edmond came to take us all to the mountains to pick out a tree for the meeting room. We dressed in winter coats, mittens, and boots. By the time we were all bundled up, we resembled astronauts heading to space.

I could barely move as we climbed into the bus.

Kyla was back on bedrest and had to stay behind. To pass the time, she and Ms. King wrapped presents and sang Christmas carols while we were gone.

Mary and Miss Adeline accompanied us on the outdoor adventure. We exuberantly sang Christmas songs.

We were no "Mormon Tabernacle Choir," but we sounded surprisingly good. Singing at the top of our lungs, we were almost hoarse by the time we arrived at the designated stop.

Eevie was first out of the bus. She instantly fell on her behind and rolled over into the snow to secretly form a snowball. As Afton climbed down the stairs, she was pelted by a snowball to her leg. Afton immediately jumped from the stairs and began forming her own pile of snowball ammunition.

By the time the other girls and I exited the bus, Eevie and Afton had a stockpile ready to attack us. We were easy targets since we had no defense.

Quickly, we scattered and built a barricade for protection. Once inside, we made our own snowballs and started throwing them at the girls. Pretty soon we were in a snowball war.

They didn't stand a chance against all of us.

When Eevie and Afton couldn't keep up anymore, Eevie came forward waving her white scarf.

"We surrender!" she cried.

Everyone laughed and threw one more snowball at her to reinforce the win. We all collapsed on the snowy ground, worn out from the fun.

Edmond quickly reminded us that we still had a tree to find and cut down.

"Okay, ladies, enough fun. It's time to get to work," I said as I let out a sigh.

Slowly, we stood up and brushed the snow from our coats.

We hiked up the mountain for about 30 minutes when Mary started yelling, waving her arms, and pointed toward one beautiful Noble Fir tree.

"I think I found it!" she exclaimed.

"It's perfect!" Everyone agreed.

Edmond brought the ax forward and began chopping down the large tree.

"Timberrrrrrrrr!" he yelled, as we listened to the tree crash onto the snow-covered earth.

It took all of us to drag the 10-foot-tall tree back to the bus through the heavy snow.

"One, two, three," we all counted in unison as we lifted the tree into the back of the bus and pushed it inside.

I picked up one last snowball and threw it directly at Eevie. Before she had the chance to retaliate, I ducked back inside the bus.

We were worn out from the day's activities and quickly fell asleep. Mary and Miss Adeline kept Edmond awake on the drive home. It was still snowing, and the roads were getting slick. He cautiously drove down the road.

I opened my eyes just in time to see the bright lights coming straight at us. Edmond swerved out of the way of an oncoming semi and landed right into a ditch.

With an abrupt halt, the bus came to a stop. The sudden jerk tossed everyone around.

"Is everyone okay?" Miss Adeline cried as she checked each and every one of the bus seats.

Some of the seats had folded in half trapping a couple of the girls underneath them. Miss Adeline helped them wiggle their way out.

A couple of young ladies complained about bumping their heads. Some had cuts on their hands and legs, but, thankfully, no one was seriously injured.

Mary instructed us to put our coats and gloves on and to wrap up in any blankets we could find. We snuggled together to stay warm.

It dawned on me that we hadn't heard anything from Edmond. I walked up to the front of the bus to check on him and found him bent over in a pool of blood.

"Help!" I screamed. "Edmond is hurt!"

I tried talking to him but got no response.

Miss Adeline came forward and gently raised Edmond's head. He was conscious but had a large deep cut on his forehead. She reached for the first aid kit stored overhead and found an ace wrap and bandages.

Miss Adeline grabbed a handkerchief from Edmond's pocket and wiped off the blood from his oozing wound. I felt a bit queasy and stepped back before throwing up into a nearby trash can.

Eevie stepped forward and helped me to a seat. Mary assisted Miss Adeline and found a thermos of water. I took a quick drink to rinse out my mouth and handed it back to Mary. They were able to rouse Edmond enough to get him to take a sip.

Decisions had to be made.

It was getting dark out, and with the bad road conditions, there wasn't much traffic on the highway.

It was decided that Miss Adeline would stay on the bus while Mary and Afton would go for help. I wanted to go but was still feeling weak and nauseated. I felt a bump on my forehead and realized I had hit my head on the window when we crashed.

Mary located the hazard lights and turned them on in hopes of someone seeing us. Then she and Afton grabbed an extra blanket and headed into the storm.

We silently said a prayer for their safety.

Edmond came around and suggested we run the bus for a few minutes to warm up. The gas gauge showed there was plenty of gas. Mary started the engine and got the heater going.

The warmth felt so good, and we savored it for the few short minutes it was on. We turned the engine off and on hoping we wouldn't run out of gas or run the battery down.

Making sure Edmond and the rest of us were safe, Mary finally sat down and discovered a large gash on her own leg.

Eevie noticed it as well and grabbed the first aid kit. After cleaning Mary's wounded leg, Eevie wrapped the remaining gauze and bandages around the cut.

"Thank you, Eevie," Mary said softly.

Some girls in the back started singing, "Silent Night." We all joined in and continued singing until we saw the flashing lights of a police car pull up beside us.

An officer got out of the car, and we soon saw the shadows of Afton and Miss Adeline inside.

Relieved, Mary greeted the officer.

"Is everyone okay in here?" the officer asked, as he climbed into the bus.

"We have some cuts and scrapes, but seem to be alright," Mary said. "Our driver, Edmond, is hurt the most."

"An ambulance is on the way, along with another bus to take you all home," the police officer told us.

Soon the ambulance arrived, and the emergency responders attended to Edmond's head. They also checked the rest of us to make sure we were okay to travel.

Edmond rode in the ambulance while the rest of us waited for the bus. It wasn't far behind, and soon we were all warm and safely on our way home.

Too tired to sing, we fell asleep.

It was nearly two o'clock in the morning before we made it home.

The police station had notified Ms. King about the situation. She and Kyla waited for us on the couch in the entry hall.

Kyla had fallen asleep, but Ms. King heard the engine of the bus and ran to greet us.

Everyone unloaded the bus, and, after gathering our personal belongings, we all went straight to bed.

Ms. King announced that classes were canceled for tomorrow.

The next morning, after a late breakfast, we unloaded the tree.

A few local men heard about the accident and came to see what they could do for us. We were grateful for the help and gave them some homemade sugar cookies to show our appreciation.

When the dinner dishes were done, we gathered in the meeting room to decorate the Christmas tree.

Earlier that day, we each made an ornament to place on the tree. Mary and Miss Adeline wrapped the tree with lights, and Ms. King carefully climbed up the ladder to place the star on top.

It was the same star she had placed on the tree since her first Christmas with the Everlys. As the finishing touch, we all tossed silver icicles on the tree in remembrance of the previous day.

Christmas was just two weeks away. A special "Visitor's Day" was planned for Christmas Eve. I was in charge of the invitations, Eevie was in charge of food assignments, Afton was in charge of the decorating crew, and Kyla was in charge of everybody!

Still instructed to stay off her feet as much as possible, Kyla gave directions from the recliner we moved into the meeting room. Her pregnant belly stuck out like a ripe watermelon in summertime. She was anxious to finally have her baby.

Mr. Campbell had located some prospective couples as the adoptive parents and delivered the profiles to Everly Hall.

Afton took advantage of the opportunity to see her father and spent a couple of hours with him. He was pleased with her continued progress and looked forward to her coming home after the holidays.

Kyla perused the files and eliminated those she didn't feel right about. Two of them struck a chord with her though. She asked Eevie, Afton, and I for our opinions.

One by one, she read the letters written to her by the prospective parents. As she read the second letter, the words of Mrs. Phillips spoke to her, and tears fell down her cheeks. We knew she had decided.

"These are the right ones," she exclaimed. "This baby belongs to them."

We held hands and cried bittersweet tears.

Invitations were mailed, and we anxiously awaited the holiday celebration. Cookies were baked, and Everly Hall looked and smelled like the gingerbread house from Hansel and Gretal.

Christmas Eve finally arrived, and families started showing up for the party. The snow had finally stopped, making traveling easier.

Every girl's parents and guests had marked their RSVP with a "Yes." Over a hundred visitors were expected to be in attendance.

I was the first to see my family.

To my surprise, Carrie Stevens was with them. Other than being on the volleyball team together, we weren't really that close.

I ran to pick up Cheyanne, who was walking now. Cody and my parents followed close behind, and Carrie stayed in the distance.

Neither of us were sure how to react, but she obviously wanted to be here. I acknowledged my family then cautiously approached her.

"Hello, Carrie," I said.

"Hello, Laramie," she said as she shuffled back and forth. "I guess you're wondering why I'm here."

"I must admit, I'm a little confused," I said as I scratched my head.

"I heard what happened to you through the grapevine and have to say I feel really bad," Carrie said. "I didn't want to be captain of the volleyball team that badly. You deserve to still be there. Now the season is over, and you had to miss it!"

"I've moved on," I said. "I realize now that none of that really ever mattered. Sure, I'm sad about not playing my senior year, but some things are more important. Like good friends."

"Well, I'd like to be your friend," Carrie said kindly.

"I'd like that very much, Merry Christmas!" I said.

I put my arm around her shoulder, and we joined my family who was already eating cookies in the meeting room.

Lilly and Cerena accompanied Afton's family. They couldn't believe how good Afton looked.

Wearing a lacey, Jessica McClintock dress, Afton was the epitome of fashion. Her long, blonde hair softly flowing over her shoulders.

"Let's go eat," Afton said as her family laughed at the irony of her statement.

Eevie got the best surprise of all. Her mother, Colleen, got permission to visit for the holiday. Eevie couldn't believe her eyes when she appeared behind Sharon and Sarah.

Colleen ran towards her with open arms. Sobbing, they embraced.

"How did this happen?" Eevie asked.

"I have been doing so well that they let me come see you," Colleen replied.

"The hearing starts next week, so my attorney asked the judge for leniency for the holiday. My hard work finally paid off."

"I got exactly what I asked for," Eevie cried as they joined the others.

Kyla was still in her room resting. Mr. and Mrs. Armstrong, along with Jordan, asked Ms. King if they could visit her.

"Of course," she answered.

Jordan knocked softly on the door.

"Come in," Kyla quietly said.

Kyla was breathing heavily and holding her back.

"What's wrong, Kyla?" her mother asked, concerned.

"I'm not really sure," Kyla said. "This pain is different from anything I've had before. Just when I think it's over, it starts again."

"How long has this been going on?" Mrs. Armstrong asked with growing concern.

"About an hour, I guess. I didn't want to interrupt the party," Kyla said.

"Well, I think the party will go on without you," Mr. Armstrong said.

Carefully lifting her off the bed, Jordan carried Kyla down the hall and out into the parking lot. Mr. Armstrong went ahead and pulled the car up close to the entrance. Mrs. Armstrong climbed in next to her husband.

We all looked on as they drove to the hospital. Eevie, Afton, and I gathered hands and whispered a prayer for our friend.

Mary took us back to the meeting room for the white elephant gift exchange. Due to the large crowd, we were divided into two circles. The numbers one through fifty-two were placed in two separate bowls, and we each drew a number out of the bowls.

Ms. King closed her eyes and chose number one. Everyone laughed, and it continued around the circle. I got fifty-two, the highest number that could be chosen.

Simultaneously, the other circle did the same. Afton and Eevie were in the other group. We purchased gifts for each other that we would exchange privately tomorrow morning.

The fun began as Ms. King unwrapped the first gag gift. It was a roll of toilet paper. The girls in our group giggled as the game continued. Each succeeding number was given the opportunity to steal a previously opened gift.

No one wanted the roll of toilet paper, but other gifts were opened revealing candy or half used perfume. Several people took advantage of the chance to upgrade to something they liked better.

Since I was last, I got to choose anything I wanted from all the gifts. Perusing the room, I chose the toilet paper.

"You never know when it might come in handy," I said as everyone roared with laughter.

Both groups finished the game and cleaned up the wrapping paper and bows. Ms. King instructed us all to join her around the Christmas tree.

With a "Ho, ho, ho," Santa Claus appeared from behind the tree. We all recognized the familiar voice of Edmond and ran towards his outstretched arms.

"Merry Christmas!" he joyfully exclaimed.

After the happy reunion, we sat around the lighted Christmas tree and once again sang "Silent Night."

******

Miles away, Kyla prepared to deliver a special gift to a couple who never thought they would have a child of their own. With one last push, Kyla gave them the most precious gift of all, a son.

With tears in her eyes, the nurse handed the baby boy to his new parents. Kyla watched from the delivery table and smiled in approval. The open end of the blanket exposed his head covered in black hair, and his triumphal cry let her know he was healthy despite coming a couple of weeks early.

Mrs. Phillips, the new mother, gave Kyla an approving look as she swaddled the newborn next to her face. Mr. Phillips put his arm around them both and cried tears of joy.

The nurse asked Kyla if she wanted to hold the baby. She nodded, and Mrs. Phillips tenderly handed the newborn to her.

With tears stinging her eyes, she looked into the newborn's eyes staring up at her.

"I love you, sweet boy," she softly whispered.

She placed a kiss on his cheek and handed him back to his mother.

"Silent Night" played over the intercom system of the hospital as the clock struck midnight.

Chapter 18: Christmas Day and New Beginnings

The phone in the office rang early Christmas morning, waking Ms. King who quickly ran to answer it.

"Merry Christmas," she answered happily.

"Same to you, may I speak with Ms. King please?" the woman on the other end of the line wasn't quite as cheery this morning.

Maybe she's crabby because she's working on Christmas, Edna thought.

"This is Ms. King. How may I help you?" she said.

"This is Nurse Haskins from Boston General Hospital," said the woman. "The Armstrongs asked me to call and inform you that Kyla had a baby boy just before midnight last night. She and the baby are doing well. The adoptive couple is here, but there is a problem. The biological father showed up this morning with his attorney."

"That is great news, well, not the part about Preston showing up, but…" Edna said, a bit flustered. "I'll be right there after I contact Mr. Campbell."

Edna phoned Mr. Campbell who quickly agreed to meet her at the hospital.

There was a knock on my door. Slowly getting out of bed, I answered it to find Miss Adeline on the other side wearing her pajamas.

"Laramie, Kyla had a baby boy last night," Miss Adeline said. "She and the baby are doing well. Ms. King has gone to the hospital to check on things,"

I noticed some hesitation in her voice.

"What's wrong?" I asked.

"Preston is there with his lawyer," she answered.

"Oh, no. That can't be good," I responded. "Let's hope for the best. For now, let's get everyone up and celebrate."

Miss Adeline went to get the others, and I put on my slippers and bathrobe. It was Christmas morning after all, and I wasn't getting dressed until I had to.

I ran to wake up Eevie and Afton. They heard the ruckus in the hall and were already awake.

"What's going on?" they questioned.

"It's Christmas!" I said. "Oh, and Kyla had a baby boy last night, and Preston is at the hospital!"

"Wow! That's a lot," Afton said.

"I think we should say a prayer," I said.

We knelt and gathered hands.

"Father in Heaven, please protect Kyla and the baby," I said. "Help Preston be kind and to make good choices. We're so grateful for the birth of Jesus and the love we share. In the name of Jesus Christ, amen."

We glanced at each other one last time, then ran to the meeting room for Christmas morning.

Mary and Miss Adeline addressed us and informed the other girls that Kyla had the baby just before midnight. She left out the details about Preston.

"Merry Christmas!" everyone shouted.

There weren't many presents to open since we celebrated with our families the day before. But most roommates and close friends had gifts to exchange.

Afton, Eevie, and I huddled under the decorated Christmas tree and shared memories of the last few months together. Some memories made us laugh, while others brought us to tears.

We decided right then that nothing would ever keep us apart. Holding hands, we vowed to always be best friends.

We exchanged our gifts. I gave them each a friendship bracelet made from extra beads I collected from the game room floor during my service hours.

Afton presented us with charm bracelets with a mini hamburger charm attached to remind us of her eating her first hamburger in a year.

Eevie handed us both a necklace with four hearts hanging from a gold chain. She had designed them and had Sharon bring them yesterday from a jewelry store in Boston.

After putting on the bracelets and necklaces, we grabbed hands and ran to the dining room for a breakfast feast of French toast covered in strawberries and whipped cream.

In the meantime, Ms. King arrived at the hospital just as Mr. Campbell drove into the parking lot. Stepping out of his car, he approached her and shook her hand.

"Merry Christmas," Edna said. "I am sorry to bother you this morning."

"Let's just get it taken care of, without too much trouble," he replied.

They drove to the hospital where they quickly got on the elevator to the second floor Maternity Ward. As they stepped out, they heard angry voices from down the hall.

The Armstrongs, along with Preston and his lawyer, James Stevenson, waited outside Kyla's room.

Preston stood there with his arms folded across his chest.

"What is going on here?" Mr. Campbell calmly asked.

"Preston is refusing to sign the adoption papers relinquishing his rights," Mrs. Armstrong said. "He wants to take Kyla to court."

"Is that right, Preston?" Mr. Campbell asked as he looked at Preston.

"Don't say a word, Preston," Mr. Stevenson said.

Mr. Stevenson turned to face Mr. Campbell.

"Preston would like to pursue custody of the baby," Mr. Stevenson said.

"That just isn't going to happen," Mr. Campbell said. "Maybe we can make some kind of arrangement with the Phillips."

Hearing their names mentioned, Mr. and Mrs. Phillips came out of Kyla's room. Kyla was inside resting while the newborn baby was asleep in the nursery.

"How can we help?" Mrs. Phillips asked.

Seeing the concern on their faces, Preston took a moment to rethink his position.

"Can I really take care of a baby?" he asked himself.

Suddenly, images of dirty diapers, late night feedings, doctor's appointments and taking a baby everywhere he went flashed through his mind.

The images overwhelmed him, and he had to sit down. Preston quickly realized the Phillips' would do a much better job as parents than he ever possibly could. It had all just been about winning and pride getting in the way of his son and his adoptive parents having the life they deserved, Preston thought.

"These are good people who will love and care for my son," he said under his breath.

Preston turned to face Mr. and Mrs. Phillips.

"I know I haven't behaved well during all of this," Preston said. "I am willing to surrender my rights as long as I can receive updates on the boy on a yearly basis until he is 18. I don't deserve any more than that. I am sorry for the grief I have caused. I will honor Kyla's wishes."

"Well, that is certainly a change of heart, Preston," Mr. Stevenson proclaimed. "Are you sure this is what you want to do?"

Preston shrugged his shoulders and looked down.

"Yeah, it's Christmas after all. Let's just get this over with," he said.

Mr. Campbell handed him the papers, and Preston quickly signed them.

"It's official then, Mr. and Mrs. Phillips, we will see you in Family Court in six months. The judge will pronounce you as the legal parents at that time," Mr. Campbell said.

Mr. and Mrs. Phillips embraced and cried tears of joy.

"Thank you, Preston. You have given us the best Christmas we could ask for," Mrs. Phillips said.

The couple returned to Kyla's room with her parents following close behind.

"That went better than expected," Edna said. "I'm going to say 'hello' to Kyla. Have a Merry Christmas, Mr. Campbell."

Mr. Campbell returned the sentiment and headed home.

Just then, snow began to fall.

Edna joined the celebration in Kyla's hospital room. Kyla was relieved that Preston agreed to sign the adoption papers.

Now she could move on.

Kyla returned to Everly Hall a few days later. We exchanged our gifts with her, and, in return, she gave each of us a framed picture of us standing in front of the pond behind Everly Hall.

We wrapped ourselves up in blankets and went outside to sit around the campfire. Snow was lightly falling as we pondered the days ahead. Within the next month, we would say "goodbye" to Everly Hall and to each other.

We were given one week off from classes over the holidays.

Our last big celebration together was New Year's Eve. We decorated like a Las Vegas casino and played card games for hours and hours.

Mary, Miss Adeline, and Ms. King made us mocktails to drink, and we donned party hats and beaded necklaces.

We turned on the black and white television someone donated to us for Christmas and watched Dick Clark's Rockin' Eve until the ball dropped on Madison Square Garden at midnight.

We counted down from ten and then shouted, "Happy New Year!"

We raised our drinks as we welcomed in 1977.

******

On January 1, 1977, I was free to walk out the doors of Everly Hall for good. I had been looking forward to this day since the day I arrived; yet, now I dreaded it.

This had become my safe place, my refuge from the storm.

This was my home with people who loved me. I could be myself and not have to impress anyone.

I was going home with high self-esteem and with the courage to stand up for myself.

Saying goodbye to my new best friends was not going to be easy. They met me in the entry hall with my parents, my siblings and Carrie.

Baby Cheyanne walked over to me and put her hands up for me to hold her. I leaned over, picked her up and hugged her tightly. I had already started crying.

Kyla came up from behind and wrapped her arms around me. We had become so close, more like sisters than friends. I would miss her the most. Sleeping alone would take some getting used to.

Eevie added to the group hug and Afton completed the embrace. Cheyanne squealed from inside all that hugging.

"Help! Let me out!" Cheyanne cried.

Wriggling her chubby little arms, my mother broke Cheyanne loose from the tangled bodies.

"It's time to go," Mr. Johnson quietly said. "The weatherman said a storm was coming."

"Oh, I know, daddy," I said. "But it's so hard to let go."

Ms. King stood nearby with the traditional graduation scrolls in her hand. She handed it to me and asked me to open it.

With my hands shaking, I took it from her and began to read.

"Laramie Johnson, in addition to completing the required courses with a 4.0 GPA, you also passed the Life Skills course and completed six months of community service. We are grateful for your unselfish attitude," I read from the scroll. "I present to you the 'Charity' award in memory of my daughter, Oakley. Always willing to do for others what they cannot do for themselves, you have become strong, independent, and ready to take on the world."

With tears streaming down my face, I turned and hugged Ms. King.

"Thank you for showing me who I can be," I said.

Among the crowd, Mary, Miss Adeline, and Edmond came to say goodbye. I gave them each a hug and reached for the hands of my best friends.

Bowing our heads, we said a prayer of gratitude and asked for protection for my family as we traveled home.

Finally, I slid into the back seat of the car my dad brought home on that dreadful night six months ago.

The words of the Eagles song rang in my ears and brought back memories of that long drive toward the unknown.

The new car smell was gone, but it felt new to me. Carrie sat in the seat next to me and placed her hand on my leg.

"It's going to be okay, I promise," she calmly said.

And I believed her.

******

Afton reached her goal weight of 112 pounds. She learned to prepare and follow a healthy, weekly menu and maintain her weight for over two weeks. She hadn't purged in nearly four months and was doing a daily exercise routine.

One week after I left, Afton's family came to take her home. Lilly, Brody, and Cerena came too. The original support group was together again. This time there would be no secrets hiding behind baggy clothes.

Afton knew she was enough and worthy of love just the way she is. She was strong, physically, and emotionally. With her loved ones by her side, she couldn't fail.

Sharon came to pick up Eevie. Little Sarah joined her.

Eevie hoped for her mother to come, but knew it was a long shot. The trial started tomorrow, and there was a lot involved in preparing for it.

Eevie had been summoned to appear in court. She was extremely nervous and knew she would have to say incriminating things about her mother. She also knew she had to tell the truth. In the long run, it was for the best.

With her mother still in jail, Eevie could stay at Everly Hall until she turned 18. However, Sharon asked for legal guardianship, so she could live with her. Eevie could attend her own high school and have easier access to visit Colleen. The courts approved, and a judge gave legal custody to Sharon. Although sad to leave Ms. King, Eevie was thrilled with the decision.

Ms. King held two graduation scrolls in her hand. The residents of Everly Hall gathered to say their farewells.

Anxious to read what it would say, Eevie reached for her scroll. The initials EW were written on the outside, so she knew which one was hers.

Eevie gently opened it.

"Evelyn Wright, having completed the required courses with a 3.2 GPA, and the Life Skills course we award you with the 'Endurance' award," she read. "You have conquered some of life's most difficult battles. You are a great example of pushing through the hard stuff and coming out a winner."

Being a biracial girl in the 1970's had its own set of challenges. Along with having a mother in jail and living in multiple foster homes, Eevie had overcome some difficult obstacles.

Ms. King hugged her tightly and nodded in approval of her success.

Afton stepped forward to accept her scroll from Ms. King.

She untied the pink ribbon wrapped around it.

"Afton Campbell, having completed the required course with a 3.6 GPA and Nutrition 101, we present you with the 'Julia Child' award," Afton read. "You have been recognized as a culinary artist not only in the kitchen but in life as you struggle each day with an illness that once held you captive."

"Congratulations, sweetheart," Miss Adeline gave her a squeeze and handed her a candy bar as a bonus. The crowd cheered and applauded.

Afton and Eevie motioned for Kyla to join them at the front. The three of them clasped hands and raised them high above their heads in celebration of this milestone.

The time had once again come to say goodbye. They bowed their heads in thanksgiving for their new and enduring friendship for the last time.

Eevie and Afton turned and walked hand in hand to their waiting families and drove away into the snowy horizon.

Since her friends had left, Kyla was left alone with her thoughts. She was still healing both physically and mentally from the delivery of her baby. She knew she had made the right choice, but she felt empty and alone.

In five months, the baby would legally belong to someone else.

Was she ready for that?

Was she ready to return to high school and resume a normal teenage life? Life would never be the same for her. A piece of her heart would always be missing.

The one constant she had was Jordan. She smiled as she thought of his goofy glasses from kindergarten. Kyla decided to call him and see how he was doing.

She hadn't heard from him since Christmas Day.

After getting permission from Ms. King to make the call, Kyla went into the office and dialed Jordan's phone number.

"Hello," he answered.

"Hi, Jordan, it's me, Kyla," she said reluctantly. "How are you?"

"Hi, Kyla. I'm well, how 'bout you?" he replied.

"I'm okay, I guess. Laramie and the others have gone home. I miss them... and you," she said.

There was a brief silence, and then Jordan spoke up.

"I miss you too," he said.

"I'm coming home soon. I'd like to see you. That is, if you want to...see...me," Kyla said.

"I would like that very much. When will you be home?" Jordan asked.

They continued talking for about fifteen more minutes when Ms. King came in and cleared her throat.

"Uhhem," she said. "I think it's time to wrap it up."

"Okay, Ms. King, I'll say goodbye," Kyla said. "I have to go, Jordan, but I'll be in touch and let you know what day to expect me."

"We'll talk soon then, goodbye," Jordan said.

Kyla hung up the phone and looked at Ms. King with her frightened eyes.

"How did you do it?" Kyla asked. "I mean, after you let your baby go. Seeing her everyday had to break your heart."

Ms. King pulled Kyla in close to her and looked her straight in the eyes.

"You never give up," Ms. King said. "You get up every morning and keep moving. Your baby is in a loving home and being cared for. It's time for you to move on and make the most of your life. It won't be easy, but it's doable. And your baby will do the same."

"Thank you, but he's not my baby," Kyla said with a teary smile. "He belongs to the Phillips, and I'm okay with that."

The two walked out hand-in-hand and turned off the light.

Epilogue

Two weeks later, Kyla returned home to find Jordan waiting on her doorstep with a bouquet of flowers.

"Welcome home!" he announced and pulled her into his chest.

She stepped back and looked him in the eyes.

"Does this mean what I think it does?" Kyla asked.

"If you mean, do I love you? Then, yes it does." Jordan smiled.

Five months later he accompanied her to the courthouse to witness the final adoption proceedings.

Mr. and Mrs. Phillips greeted her with open arms and allowed her to hold little Matthew. He smiled as she looked into his eyes.

It was perfect.

Kyla and Jordan finished their senior year, and both graduated with honors. Following graduation, they attended Boston University.

Jordan pursued his law degree at Harvard. The two married and had three girls. Kyla was a stay-at-home mom, and Jordan became a family law attorney.

Afton finished her junior and senior year of high school. She studied nutrition at a local college and helped girls with eating disorders. On occasion, she visited Everly Hall and shared her story of survival. She maintained her friendship with Cerena and Lilly.

Colleen Wright was convicted on two accounts of involuntary manslaughter. The judge considered her time served for her drug charges and gave her a set five years in prison with parole offered in two years.

She was determined to get out of jail and spend quality time with Eevie. Although she couldn't make up for time lost, she could make the most of the future.

Two years later, Colleen was released on good behavior.

Eevie lived with Sharon for her last two years of high school. Sharon eventually adopted Sarah.

By the time Eevie graduated, Colleen was released, and the two of them did some traveling together.

Colleen became a drug addiction counselor, and Eevie worked at a thrift store.

I went back to high school and finished my senior year. My old friends tried to pull me back into their games, but Carrie stood by me and supported me.

Shoplifting nearly ruined my life, but thanks to Mrs. King, I learned from my mistakes.

We all grew up during our time at Everly Hall. We were taught life skills through example and daily living. We were taught honesty, integrity, loyalty, and love.

We were taught to be kind and to serve others. We were taught to be the best version of ourselves and to treat others with respect.

Edna King, the woman responsible for joining us all in friendship, was a stellar lady. She didn't just tell us how to live, she showed us.

Five years after leaving Everly Hall, we reunited at Edna King's funeral service. Although she never said a word, Ms. King had a chronic sore throat and cough.

That explained why she often cleared her throat before speaking. We just thought it was to get our attention. She was diagnosed with throat cancer and eventually succumbed to its devastating effects.

Georgia and Francis Everly started something big. Edna King kept their dream alive and I, Laramie Johnson, will continue the legacy.

Acknowledgements

This book would not have been possible without the help of so many.

First of all, thank you to my husband, Jeff, for taking me to Vermont, Maine, Massachusetts and New Hampshire to see the colorful fall foliage. Our adventures led us to a lodge where I received my inspiration for this book. I didn't know until then what story I had to share.

My thanks also go out to my sisters, Jeanne and Joy, for their constant support and willingness to share their thoughts with me. Without knowing it, I brought back life memories of heartache and healing. They are my best friends and cheerleaders.

Thanks also to my sweet, oldest granddaughter, Brayli. She has been my proofreader and sidekick from the beginning. She came to know my characters and was able to capture them perfectly in her sketches. I will always cherish the bond we formed in the making of this book.

Thank you to my editor, Lisa Dayley-Smith. As childhood friends in Sunday School, we never would have imagined our lives being connected by our love of writing over 50 years later. Fate brought us back together to share this journey and rekindle a cherished friendship. Lisa is the author of her own book, "The Frozen Trail."

Lastly, thank you to all the girls who have ever touched my life: my beautiful daughters, who show me strength and endurance everyday by their examples, my mother and mother-in-law who overcame hard things by faith and raised their children with unconditional love and patience, my sisters-in-law who treat me like family and support my children, and to all of my girlfriends who helped me to recognize what true friendship looks like.

Made in the USA
Monee, IL
05 November 2023

45804615R00116